Praise for Dwelling and Learning to Love a Forest

The poems in this book are rooted in a forest place… Reading, your intuitive wandering will be spangled with glimpses of forest light to restore you from exile back to your forest home.~*Kim Stafford*, former Oregon Poet Laureate, author of Singer Come from Afar

Learning to Love a Forest exquisitely captures how the forest can teach… Bill's writing inspires life-loving consciousness and gifts us with a powerful teaching for protecting nature, a gateway to personal action, and a beam of light on nature's will to live. ~*Fran Teplitz*, Executive Co-Director, Green America

In Learning to Love a Forest Hutchins shares a portal to connection, quietude and love. If you've never loved a forest this book may show you how
Krista Schlyer, environmental advocate, photographer / filmmaker

Dwelling is multi-faceted. It is poetry and prose. It offers medicine for the spirit, ideas for the mind, exercises for the body, and tools for the hands. It is a great guide for dreamers, planners, doers, and celebrators! ~*Emily Gupta*

Dwelling invited me to stop and dwell - within myself, within my body, within the spaces of my home. ~*Anne Dykers*

Dwelling brings a purposeful consideration to the entire endeavor [of ecological living], opening the door for conscious living, design, building and development that holds inner and outer worth of all things as paramount. ~*Lourdes Barden-Sims*

DWELLING

BILL HUTCHINS

ISBN: 979-8-9992568-6-7

Material in this book was previously published in two volumes, under the following titles and International Standard Book Numbers:

DWELLING: A Poetic Exploration of Home, ISBN: 978-1-62429-151-7
DWELLING: Learning to Love a Forest, ISBN: 978-1-62429-354-2

Cover Image by Kelly VanDellen / Istock 2105376113

SLIGO CREEK PUBLISHING
9039 SLIGO CREEK PARKWAY
SILVER SPRING, MARYLAND 20901
SLIGOCREEKPUBLISHING.COM

To Kate, Henry, and Richard

Table of Contents

The goal of awakening love in the human being and giving life here on Earth a more spiritual meaning need to be fulfilled; otherwise, it won't be possible to sustain the human race here for very long.

– Sri Prem Baba

We too can offer something to you: our experience and the knowledge that has come from it. The specific experience I'm talking about has given me one certainty: consciousness precedes being... For this reason, the salvation of this human world lies nowhere else than in the human heart, in the human power to reflect, in human meekness and in human responsibility. Without a global revolution in the sphere of human consciousness, nothing will change for the better in the sphere of our being as humans, and the catastrophe toward which this world is headed — be it ecological, social, demographic or a general breakdown of civilization — will be unavoidable.

– Vaclav Havel, when President of the Czech Republic,
from a speech to the U. S. Congress

DWELLING

I am, as the rose, unfurling through Your Love.

How I Came to This Work

Life is constantly offering possibilities, many of which we avoid. Some are vital and we have no choice — they make their urgency known by the pain that accompanies them. So it was as I went through a divorce in 1991 (we separated the day after my daughter's, Kate, second birthday). I was a young professional living in a world that I wasn't, trying to find my place. I was doing everything I could contrive to avoid my soul's birthing pains. I was even willing to hold onto a marriage that served neither of us.

Our separation was decided the day before I traveled to work on a project. While I was away my wife moved out with Kate. I returned on a cold night, late. Entering the house, the ground floor appeared little changed. As I walked upstairs and looked down the hall into Kate's room, I saw nothing. It was empty, and I finally saw my own emptiness. I had no choice how to respond.

My home was a bungalow with a central hearth. I spent that winter cloistered away, held by the fire, entering the fire, learning to love the ashes.

There I was, an architect — really a poet who writes with space and form — finally exploring my inner Home. The path was (is) inclusive — many sources, all centered on Rumi and Mystical Christianity, two wings of a bird. And the way led to many understandings, rotating around the vision that our life's journey is a process of finding our spiritual Home, in part, through our physical home. This process is Dwelling.

My greatest teacher was Kate. Young children say YES! to life, they demand to be known and to know — to love is to know, all of it, without judgment, with devotion. They're fearless; they're unconsciously one with their source; they see everything being alive, inviting a response — they're a spring flower, bursting through the soil. One day I was sitting on the floor, in a depressed-stupor, when Kate grabbed me, shook me, and said,

"Daddy, get up and play!"

So I slowly rose through the soil of my grief — the divorce was only the iceberg's tip — taking the time to taste each layer. I explored my way through spiritual texts, meditation, poetry, being in nature, dance, and playing with Kate, the fruit of which evolved into Dwelling.

Kate recently read Rainer Maria Rilke's *Letters to a Young Poet* — "Everything you ever said to me is in that book!" I found Rilke's book early on during my awakening, which runs a parallel track with Kate's life. Dwelling has grown within me these many years — I only now realize — as an account of my dialogue with Rilke. His words are a spring flowing through a small opening on a hillside, covered with watercress, nurturing and giving life to my searching.

Prose Note to The Reader

Dwelling offers ways of living more fully in our home and place, inspired by poetic images of our spiritual Home. Poetry offers life-giving images, comes from the core, reveals our deeper humanity — can be spiritual. *Dwelling* then begins with poetry, explored in Book 1, and becomes tangible in Books 2 & 3. If poetry doesn't speak to you, please forgo Book 1. Books 2 & 3 will give you ways to Dwell. Book 4 is pure earth love,

Regarding the title page quote, below the rose, I received this line in a dream, where I was listening to Coleman Barks — who has beautifully brought us Rumi's poetry — being interviewed. I experience my dream life as no different from my waking hours — I just assumed I heard the interview while awake. I asked Coleman about the line, and he said it wasn't his.

Regarding the photos — they are images of our beautiful earth, our home, as it was given to us in the beginning. The force of this beauty inspires awe, respect, and a desire to cherish every drop. These moments open us to receive Spirit's touch — Love — in our hearts. We can create such openings in the making, and living in, our homes. This is *Dwelling*.

The photos are not metaphors. They explore how our human impulses are found in the beauty of the earth; or how our human impulses come from the energies and power of the earth; or there is no separation between us and the earth, Her creatures and the cosmos.

When one of us sees a glimmer of light, we exclaim to our companions that perhaps we see a way out of the darkness. So is *Dwelling* offered to you.

A few notes regarding the text:

- Spirit — the word I'll use as logos for our spiritual Source, which, being ineffable and personal, I'm leaving open for you to name.
- Home — our inner, spiritual origin; our deep, still center, united with all; where Spirit resides.
- home — our heart, physical home, and the earth.
- Light — Spiritual Light, a conduit for Love.
- light — sunlight.
- Love — the nectar we live for, our Union.
- Self — our spiritual Self, who resides in our Home.
- self — our human self, with all of our wounds, karma, and beautiful imperfections.
- Membrane — unites that which it seems to separate.
- In Book 1, poems by other poets are justified along the left edge of the page. My writings are centered on each page. Italicized parts in my writings are from previous poems by others.
- The mandala on page 15 is found on the well cover in Glastonbury, England. The well embodies the divine feminine, and is revered by all faiths. The garden it resides in is a World Peace Garden.

Poetic Note to The Reader

Dwelling is kaleidoscopic, seeking to illuminate
Through the endlessly faceted Home logos.
I've shared what has shined through me.

This book grows,
Spiraling out from its seed-center.

I begin by giving you a seed for Dwelling,
Followed by poetic images of Home,
To inspire your Dwelling.

Then I give you
Some ways to Dwell,
For you to plant and tend your own garden.

The last part offers a few forms
Dwelling takes as it's lifting out of the earth
To further incarnate.

Every page sits in silence.

May my words be a wood thrush's song
Somewhere, somewhat hidden,

Invitations for you to engage with
On your way Home.

Exploring Dwelling is an unfolding —

Through holding the door open,
Inviting friends to come, listen
To the music
And sing with me.
Many voices fill the air — I invite you to join us.
(See the note regarding our website at the end of *Dwelling*)

BOOK I

Poetic Exploration of Dwelling

A SEED FOR DWELLING

Exploring the Core of Living in Spirit's
Love and Light

Our home is our center of refuge, a portal into our Home.

Spirit's life-force, Love-force
Is within everything, as turbulence in the sky —
Unseen, Spirit shakes us, awakens us
While it fills our soul.

Our heart is our soul-opening for Spirit.

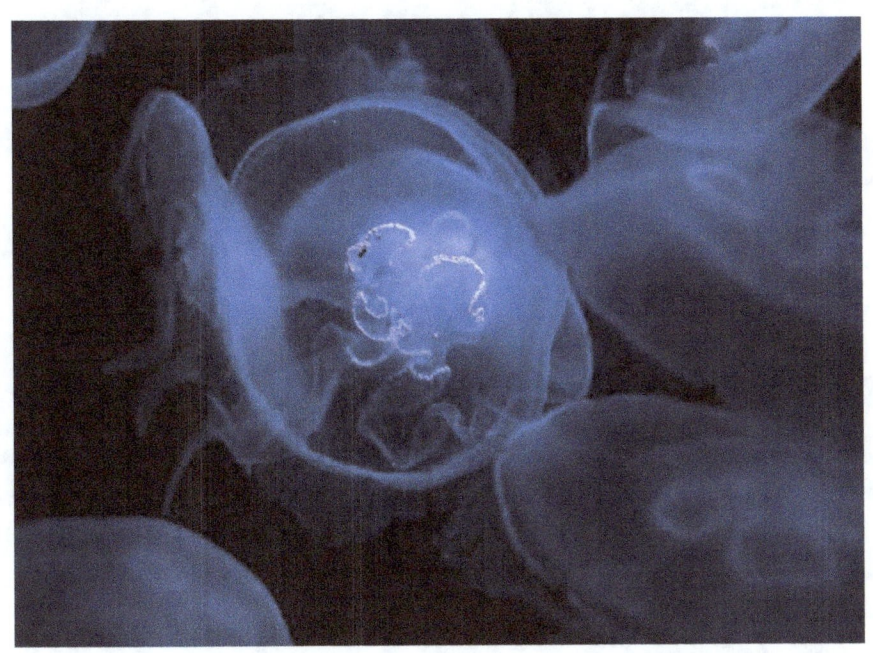

There is a light grain seed inside.
You fill it with yourself, or it dies.

I'm caught in this curling energy! Your hair!
Whoever is calm and sensible is insane!
    – Rumi

We are born with, and always carry within us A light grain seed, holding
The mysteries — logos — of the cosmos.

Our seed is our Home.
Our home is our Home chalice.

We are given freedom
To choose to live through sprouting our seed,
To fill it with our Self.

Dwelling is a way to say yes.

We can consider our life as a journey to find Home.

Home lies in spiritual realms,
Yet paradoxically
Here we are, living in this material plane,
In our world's illusion —

Everything is a mental construct
Other than our bodies, the earth and the stars.

We are incarnate beings —
With each step we're looking for and wanting
To know our connection
With where we're from.

We came from our Home, and
In the end, we'll return Home.

For now, wanting Union with our Source,
We can create thresholds into Spirit

Where we find our Home.

The things we live with can be doors into spiritual realms.

Consider a single candle in a dark room —
It gives itself to create light, and
It illuminates our center.
It resonates a vibration of deep peace.
It glows silence, creating space
To see beyond the material plane.

Our home can be a candle amidst darkness.

13

14

There are endless ways to create an opening into Spirit.
What they all require — mindfulness.

Anything can take us into deeper realms
But only through our heart-centered,
Conscious, imaginative engagement
In the moment.

Think young child —
Everything is alive to them.

Before mindfulness, there is belief —
Belief opens us
To be in relationship with Spirit.

We live the life we believe,
Including across the threshold.

We are not human beings having a spiritual experience,
We are spiritual beings having a human experience.
— Pierre Teilhard de Chardin

You don't have to believe in God to experience Spirit.

There are deeper, eternal life forces
That animate the material realm we live in,
That we can engage with by Dwelling.

We are portals for Spirit to enter the world.
We can co-create.

Spirit's fruit is LOVE.
Spirit's LIGHT illuminates all.

To be rich is to not want.

We can live in peace, in Union, With only a bowl and a candle.

Or less.

We have everything, yet we're tempted
To keep consuming, hoping
We'll eventually find that thing which will make us whole.

This leads to spiritual impoverishment.

What we want is free, and is not a thing.

All we need is provided by the earth.

Life-force pulsates within Her, and all Her aspects.
The earth offers Herself to our body, mind and soul, yet
Our mother is not a resource to consume.

The secrets of the cosmos are all around us, here,
Incarnated in the earth.

Every answer lies before us.

Artists and children teach us to see.
Once we open our eyes
Everything is alive —

We can find our way Home.

Our heart is a crystal
Where resides a pure, divine Light-being —

Light grain seed —

Holding and refracting Spirit's Light
To give to our companions.

The clearer we are, the more deeply Light
Unites us, heart to heart.

Through Love, Light expands.

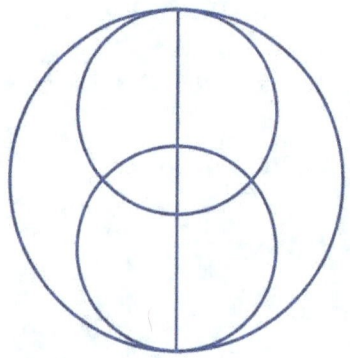

We can live here
In the space that unites apparent opposites,
In the realm of paradox,
In the curl of the wave
Where the ocean's Love-energy meets our shore.

Aligned with Spirit, which runs
Through the spine of us all.

All held within the ineffable.

Images of Home For Dwelling

These images are offered as doors to enter
for your way Home.

Home and home
The Heart of Dwelling

Soul : Heart : home : Earth : Cosmos

Our deepest presence is the Love-energy
That runs through the spine of all dimensions.

This is our Home.

Each realm mirrors and is in dialogue with the others —
Acting in one affects all.

Life's vitality, Light-filled Love, comes into our being
Through the spaces of our
Heart, home, and earth.

How can we embrace our sorrow
Or learn how to love or
See what we lose when we die?

Only Your song, over the earth
Honors our life and makes it holy.
                    – Rainer Maria Rilke

Our heart is a crucible, attuned to Spirit's song —

Taking in all of life, our joy and pain,
Allowing us to be in authentic relationship
With our companions —

Honoring our life and making it holy.

Our home

Firmly plants our body in the earth
As it reaches our spirit to the sky
It expands us along the earth's atmosphere
To all things.

Our home is where we make Home

Our home is a vessel to hold love;

It's our sanctuary, where
We can open to deeper realms:

It's our place of vulnerability,
Where we're free to live
In truth, and honestly respond.

.

Our home receives all of our emotions,
Is a vessel to pour our whole being into.

Our home is our safe enclosure for all of our
Many selves—aspects of our soul—to express themselves;

Our home contains our seeds of constant renewal,
Where we can live in simple devotion
With the gift of life.

We're never alone; we're always Home.

**Today, like every other
day, we wake up empty and
frightened. Don't open the
door to the study
and begin reading. Take down a musical instrument.**

**Let the beauty we love be what we do.
There are hundreds of ways to kneel and kiss the ground.**
      –Rumi

The beauty we love
Are the spaces of our Home And is who we are—

Our Self—

Resides in our Home
And comes to light through humility.

Our Great Paradox
Balancing Our Wings

Our great paradox

Is that Home is to be found only within ourselves,
At our still center, yet we make Home
By living in and through this world.

Our knowing of our Home is essential
Given the despair and anguish we encounter
Doing our work within our world crisis.

We, and our home
Can be a calm center
Within a hurricane.

Our voice in the world bears riper fruit
As our heart-crystal-center is clarified.

Yin —

Mother　　　moon　　　protector —

Refuge　　　　　intimacy —

Private　　　self —

Belonging —

Feminine　　soft　　curve　　womb —

Familiar　　comfortable　　tradition, ancestry —

Mud　　settling　　silence, stillness —

Careful　　　　go with the flow —

Rest, secure　　　　fluidity　　　light —

Protective　　receptive —

River　　searching —

Earth　　humble　　oriented —

Balance　　asymmetry　　space —

Contraction　　into ourselves　　listening —

In-ward —

CLOSED —

— Yang

— Father   sun   inspirer

— Expansion   immensity

— Public   community

— Wandering

— Masculine   hard   straight   phallus

— Unknown   challenging   progressive

— Chaos   interaction

— Risk-taking   willful

— Growth   movement   solidity

— Confronting   projecting

— Tree   being rooted, grounded

— Sky   ego   exploring

— Dynamic   asymmetry   structure

— Expansion   out to other realms   engaging

— Out-ward

— OPEN

Our knowing of Home rises out of the energy
Generated through living into the creative tension of life.

Entering into paradox reveals The Middle Way,

Where we can find the resolution of and balanced response
To the seemingly contradictory dual nature of all things.

Our life's journey is made real

As we Dwell in the overlapping space
Between complimentary possibilities.

The grief of what you've lost
lifts a mirror up to where you are bravely working.
Expecting the worst, you look up
and instead here's the joyful face you've been wanting to see.

Your hand opens and closes
and opens and closes.
If it were always a fist or always stretched open
you would be paralyzed.

Your deepest presence is in every small expanding and contracting,
the two as beautifully balanced and coordinated as bird wings.
       – Rumi

Our compulsions and addictions arise
When we reverse the direction of this dynamic —
When we seek Home in this world
Rather than through this world.
This paradox is the genesis of

Our grief —
That this world does not hold
The essence of what makes us whole;

And our joy —
That there is an ineffable loving-mystery
Which is our birthright and accessible
If we ask for it and enter into paradox.

If we have the courage and will to find it there.
We do.

Spirit's Fruit is Love
Bearing the Beams of Love

And we are put on earth a little space
That we might learn to ear the beams of love.
        – William Blake

We learn to bear the beams of love
By asking and living into

The questions

That take us to our true Self,
Such as the ones that the death of a loved one
Or the birth of our child raise;

That get to the truth of our existence,
That takes us into our basic human impulses
That flow through the blood of us all,

That forms the membrane of our heart.

35

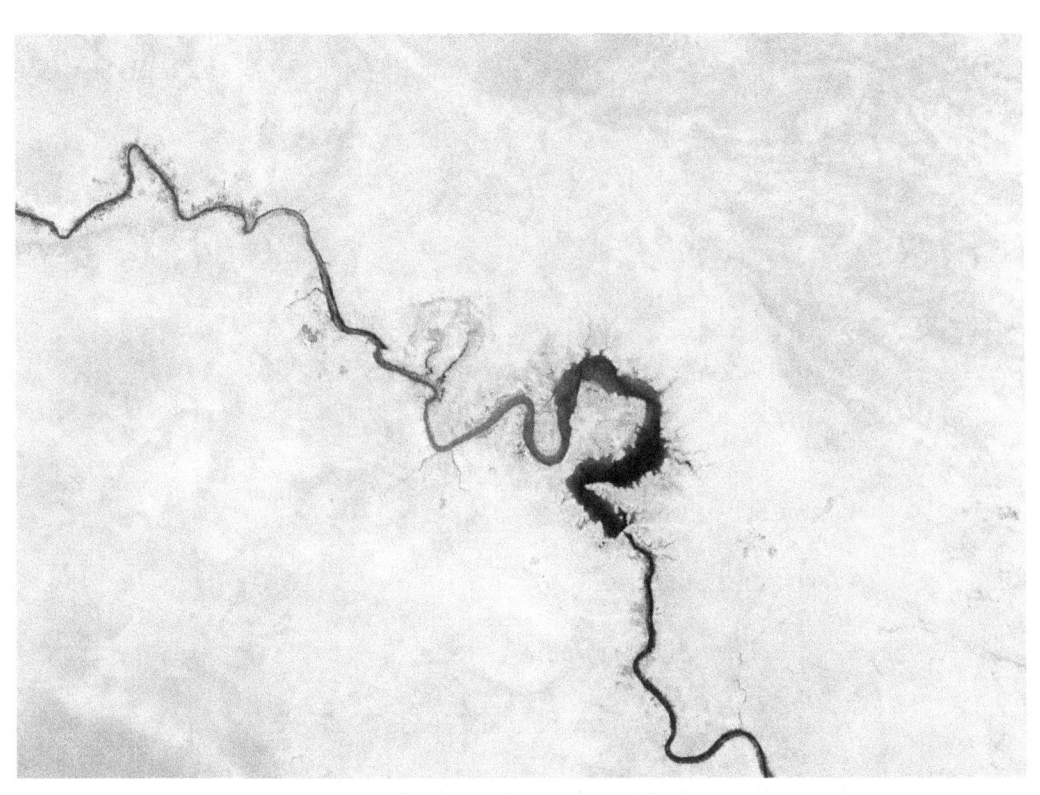

Have I loved well?

How do I express the Love that I am?

Why did I incarnate…..what did I come here to do?

What gave me joy as a child?

What really matters?

What is the truth of reality?

How do I live into that truth?

What am I to do with my pain and sense of alienation?

What will I want when on my deathbed?

Self-Portrait

It doesn't interest me if there is one God
or many gods.
I want to know if you belong or feel
abandoned,
if you can know despair or see it in others.
I want to know
if you are prepared to live in the world
with its harsh need
to change you. If you can look back
with firm eyes,
saying this is where I stand. I want to know
if you know
how to melt into that fierce heat of living,
falling toward
the center of your longing. I want to know
if you are willing
to live, day by day, with the consequence of love
and the bitter
unwanted passion of your sure defeat.

I have been told, in that fierce embrace, even
The gods speak of God.
            – David Whyte

Our despair rises out of our lack of faith.

We don't know and believe we are loved,
That we are known and cherished, deeply, beyond
The changing weather of our companion's emotions.

Everything we need is here.

It is our life's work to
Fall toward the center of our longing. To plant our self where we are, and say

"I am here."

To be still, listen, and
Know Spirit
Is in every fiber of us, and our place.

Those who don't feel this Love
pulling them like a river,
Those who don't drink dawn
like a cup of spring water
or take in sunset like supper,
Those who don't want to change,

Let them sleep.

This Love is beyond the study of theology,
that old trickery and hypocrisy.
If you want to improve your mind that way,

Sleep on.

I've given up my brain.
I've torn the cloth to shreds
and thrown it away.
If you're not completely naked,
Wrap your beautiful robe of words
around you,

And sleep.
          – Rumi

We do not find our way talking about spirituality.
We're being invited to
Tear off those clothes, get naked, and live!

Life is a process of awakening
To the Love we are.

We can live into the truth of each moment,
Face honestly and courageously our difficult questions,
Be and give the Love we are
In each space — relationship — we enter.

We can see and praise and take hold of —
With endless gratitude —
The precious gift being offered.

Our purpose and work becomes clearer and grows
With each intentional step we take.

As we grow in compassion —
We are all suffering —
Our capacity to love deepens.

Space —

That within our heart,
        Or between two beings,
                Or a being and a place —

Is the medium in which Love arises.

We fall IN Love;
All relationships are doors into Love.

Each relationship expands us
Out of our small mental-box
Into Love's spaciousness.

43

A touch

A simple loving press against our tender flesh

Is the catalyst for the Love-energy
That flows through and unites
The stars and planets and oceans and land and skies
And all creatures.

Everything meaningful
Is formed through relationship, Ignited by a touch.

Results and things
Do not have any significance in themselves —
They are only a finger pointing to the moon.

The moon's luminosity is what we seek.

It's not the vessel we live for, rather for what is inside.
The seed holds life, not the husk.

Our body is temporal; Love is eternal.

Relationships are containers for actions
And all actions are a form of touching.

Including our thoughts.

Our thoughts go before us
And fill each space we enter.
This is our deeper dialogue, as
The oceans currents affect the winds.

Expanding Our Vital Center
Breathe Into Me

There is some kiss we want
with our whole lives,
The touch of Spirit on the body.

Seawater begs the pearl
to break its shell.
And the lily, how passionately
it needs some wild Darling!

At night, I open the window
and ask the moon to come
and press its face against mine.
Breathe into me.

Close the language-door,
and open the love-window.
The moon won't use the door,
only the window.
              – Rumi

Spirit's imperative to fill us
Enters when we open our heart and ask for it —

Breathe Into Me.

Each breath is an invitation to live
As it gives us the vitality to live well.
With each breath

Our senses and awareness expand —
With attention we connect
With life's deeper rhythms.

The rhythm of our breath holds
Echoes of our ocean existence

And mirrors the pulse of the cosmos.

Each breath carries with it an "Ah!"
Of exaltation, feeling a part of everything;
And of exile, feeling our sure defeat.

We can trust darkness.

Every living thing grows from darkness.
We are continually breaking out of darkness

Into Light.

Fear not — death is a birth,
Taking us back Home.

The Swan

This clumsy living that moves lumbering
as if in ropes through what is not done,
reminds us of the awkward way the swan
walks.
And to die, which is the letting go
of the ground we stand on and cling to every
day,
is like the swan when he nervously lets himself
down
into the water, which receives him gaily
and which flows joyfully under
and after him, wave after wave,
while the swan, unmoving and marvelously
calm,
is pleased to be carried,
fully grown,
more like a king, further and further on.
        – Rilke

The path to freedom,

Union with our Source,
Is surrendering.
Our life is a series of deaths
Ascending the steps to the temple.
We just need to let
Our self
Down
Into
To be carried by
    The water.
The water is our Home.
The spaces of our home beg us to crack open
And give voice to our Self.

Our home forms our shell,
Which holds our water
Waiting to be opened.

We can become more alive
Each day as we Dwell in our home —
Just as when
playing
In the snow or the surf.

Each moment more awake, moment by moment.

Our Heart's First Layer of Home
Our Body is a Vessel for Love to Enter

My lover is to me a sachet of myrrh resting between my breasts.
– Song of Songs, 1: 13

Our Home is the realm of deep intimacy between

The Lover — Spirit,
And the beloved — us.

We are spiritual beings that incarnate in our body.
As a chalice holds a sacrament
So our body holds Spirit's

Light grain seed.

Our body is an instrument singing our Light-song.

Our body provides our primal means of being in the world —
It's the membrane
Through which the journey of our soul is played.

The spaces and forms of our body,
And how we engage
With our companions and the earth with our body,
Establishes the basis for all relationships.

All that surrounds us holds within it
Reverberations of our inner presence
As we are in their vibration-fields,
Uniting us with our companions and place.

Out of each meeting rises a space, thresholds to our Union.

From there unfurls our journey Home —
Of our opening our self
For another to enter into, of the growing intimacy
And coming together of lovers.

Love is our Union.

Our Source is Love. We are Love. We are One.
We can live in knowing this.

When we open our hearts, Love flows into and from us —
Vapor rises from our heat, from heart to heart
Condensing into another Light-giving heart-crystal facet.

Through Love, Light expands.
As Light expands, we burn off the fog
To further know our Union

And create the world in Love.

Our consummate opening, making love

Is our deepest sense of coming Home in our material existence —
Being filled with the eternal life-force
Through the consecration intimate space offers.

Making love is our greatest act of co-creation —
Making a new life
That every action can be.

(Making love is only sex
When we're not aligned with our Source.)

Our home expands our physiology —
The next layer of enclosure rippling out from our heart,
Giving further form to our Home.

Our life-force is
Simultaneously centrifugal and centripetal —

Our heart is a microcosm of the cosmos
And its layers of enclosure extend infinitely,
Interconnecting with all other beings.

The cosmos completes our heart.
Our heart completes the cosmos.

Dwelling in Our home
The Healing Power of Space

Creating and living in our home builds our soul.

That which we seek within ourselves
Finds form in how we make our home.

The spaces of our home can elicit repose,
Just as being in nature's embrace.

Repose allows us to enter our heart space
And it is through engaging in our heart space
That we find the healing for which our soul longs.

We move along our path to Home.

The spaces we enter in our home
Can be healing pools to immerse our self.

In a wondrous play of light and shadow
The deepest recesses of our soul
Slowly materialize and take shape
As gently and articulately
As the forms made by a pebble dropped into still water.

Our soul, the pebble, and the cosmos, the pool,
Become One
In silent communion.

Our home can hold
Spaces and walls that resonate
Peace and truth and beauty,
Permanence and substance and authenticity,
Simplicity and joy and balance.

These revelations of Home
Reach deeper than idle comfort and transcend style.

Our home's deeper presence is formed from nature —

Spaces filled with light and sound and color
Which gives life to walls made of real materials
With scale, proportion, rhythm, form and texture
Attuned to our deepest human impulses.

Their expression can be a medium for us
To unleash the animation within our soul.

When we align ourselves
With and act as a conduit for the eternal life-force,
A word, a slab of stone, a timber of wood —

The gifts of our earth

Further unfold their healing power.

We can reveal and give expression
To the images in our
Dreams, memories, beliefs and ancestry —

Shimmering rays of Home.

Dwelling through our home
Can be a way of giving expression
To those parts of us that lie dormant and forgotten
Through the hard and painful work of one's life —
We long for their re-integration into our lives.

This is healing.

Ecology
Making Home

Ecology

Is the mysterious process of making Home.

(Eco, the Greek root, means home.
Logos is an eternal life-force revealing itself to us)

We make Home through the practice
Of taking hold of the sacredness within all things;
By beholding the earth
As centered in the Great Mystery.

The earth is not a resource to be used —
It's a holder of Spirit to be lived with.

The spaces of our home can embody
The meeting of our self with the earth —
Our source, the living organism

In which we are.

The eternal life-force enlivens and communicates
Through the earth.

The dream of the earth —
Her story within the cosmic vision —
Comes through the endless stream
Of creation's voice.

We human beings, who in every fiber and breath
Are of the earth, and each other —
As sand particles on the Ocean's beach —
Are a part of Her dream.

We're here to co-create
The cosmic vision with the earth.

We of blood and flesh and bones have been given the capacity
To hear and respond to the cosmos' deeper rhythms.

The power

That is at our center is the same power
That explodes a star to shoot across the sky.

Blessed are the meek,
For they will inherit the earth.
— **Matthew 5: 5 NIV**

Aligned with the One are the humble, those submitted to God's will.....
They shall be open to receive the splendor of the earth's fruits and...
Strength from the universe.
— **Matthew 5: 5 from the Aramaic,**
as presented in Prayers of the Cosmos

I am so small, I can barely be seen
How can this great Love be inside me?
— **Rumi**

Dwelling grounds and incarnates our spirituality

Through our relationships
With the earth and our companions. Without humility
We negate the presence of the earth and her creatures
And we're destructive
Of one another and our source of life.

Only by being small can we know the Greatness.

Wild Geese

You do not have to be good.
You do not have to walk on your knees
for a hundred miles through the desert, repenting.
You only have to let the soft animal of your body
love what it loves.
Tell me about despair, yours, and I will tell you mine.
Meanwhile the world goes on.
Meanwhile the sun and clear pebbles of the rain
are moving across the landscapes,
over the prairies and the deep trees,
the mountains and the rivers.
Meanwhile the wild geese, high in the clean blue air,
are heading home again.
Whoever you are, no matter how lonely,
the world offers itself to your imagination,
calls to you like the wild geese, harsh and exciting —
over and over announcing your place
in the family of things.

          — Mary Oliver

Most of us know
A loving presence when in nature.

We find refuge as we feed and nurture ourselves
With that which we are from.

We learn our place.

Our soft animal of our body knows what it loves.
Open to that.
It can be messy, but it holds life.

There is deep healing in connecting
With the loving energy of the earth —
She is waiting for us to receive Her, and respond,
So that we may take another step

Towards Home.

The Creative Impulse
Becoming...Real

Making Home is our way of becoming REAL,

Which, as the Velveteen Rabbit was told by the hobby horse,
Only comes through

Life's constant vigorous rubbing.

Our experiences are without power or connection
To what we desire unless
We can give our whole self to life's rubbing.

We can engage with all of life and co-create.

Just as a mountain is pushed out
Through the body of the earth
By its deep source, so is our Self.

We become our Self

By surrendering
To our Source, letting it crack open
Our old stories and false mental constructs.

At the same time, we're being ground down
By the winds and rain, the pains and joys
Of our daily living.

This is the ebb and flow of living in
Transformative molten lava.

Consciousness precedes being…..
        - Vaclav Havel

The illusions of our world reverses this dynamic,

Encouraging us to buy fancy things
That then expresses who we are,
Based on arbitrary societal values.

These trappings of our cultural denial
Keep us asleep
As they are falsely projected
As superseding our relationship with Spirit.

We can resist the illusions dominant culture uses
To fuel its all-consuming ways —

Eternal youth, perfection, sterile cleanliness, materialism, idealism,
Insipid comfort, purity, convenience, money as the basis of culture,
Glorification of violence, romantic love as a normative condition.
The imperfect is our paradise.

Note that, in this bitterness, delight,
Since the imperfect is so hot in us,
Lies in flawed words and stubborn sounds.

> — Wallace Stevens,
> *The Poems of Our Climate*

Imperfection is essential for a vibrant world.

Just as our planet needs biodiversity
Humanity needs all ways of being.

Are we all not disabled in some way?
We're actually abled into our uniqueness.

Our Self likely takes form outside of normal.

With all of the voices telling us who to be,
It takes work to become our Self.

Whoever is calm and sensible
Is insane.

Poetry

And it was at that age...Poetry arrived
in search of me. I don't know, I don't know where
it came from, from winter or a river.
I don't know how or when,
no they were not voices, they were not
words, nor silence,
but from a street I was summoned,
from the branches of night,
abruptly from the others,
among violent fires
or returning alone,
there I was without a face
and it touched me.

I didn't know what to say, my mouth
could not speak,
my eyes could not see
and something ignited in my soul,
fever or unremembered wings
and I went my own way,
deciphering that burning fire
and I wrote the first bare line,
bare, without substance, pure
foolishness, pure wisdom
of one who knows nothing,

and suddenly I saw
the heavens
unfastened and open,
planets, palpitating plantations,
shadow perforated,
riddled
with arrows, fire and flowers,
the winding night, the universe.
And I, infinitesimal being,
drunk with the great starry
void,
likeness, image of
mystery,
felt myself a pure part
of the abyss,
I wheeled with the stars,
My heart broke loose on the wind.
      — Pablo Neruda

Our self is a fluid possibility
That we create.

Our life is different once we go our own way,
When we write our first bare line —
We may see the heavens unfasten and open.

Our longings point to where we need to go —
They tell us what is intensely missing,
Where our unremembered wings lie,
Which embers are waiting to be ignited into flames.

As a dog's cry for its master,
Our longings are our connection
To the peace and wholeness we seek.
Our longings are our power, our heart-juice —

They hold our gift to unravel,

Our flow of molten lava waiting to
Burst through
The world's illusions.

The Road Home

An ant hurries along the threshing floor with its wheat grain,
Moving between huge stacks
Of wheat, not knowing the abundance all around. It thinks its
One grain is all there is to
Love. So we choose a tiny grain to be devoted to. This body,
One path or one teacher. Look
Wider and farther. The essence of every human being can see,
And what that essence-eye takes
In, the being becomes. Saturn. Solomon! The ocean pours
Through a jar, and you might say it
Swims inside the fish! This mystery gives peace to your
Longing and makes the road home Home.
         — **Rumi**

Dwelling is a way of becoming what we behold.

We create our reality —
What we really see, deciphering that burning fire.

Our life is limitless —

In silence
We commune with our unfathomable depths;

With our imagination
We activate the passionate unfurling of our soul's song.

We smolder within when we fearfully
Hold on to our lame self and our
Self isn't lived into.

Dwelling makes the road *home Home*.

We're born with an imperative
As powerful as a river's quest to its ocean,

Being drawn by its Source.

Oppression of our journey comes from within and without.
We either implode or die when we can't flow through life's wounds.

We need to find the courage —
It's there —
To walk into and through the wounded parts of our self.

Our wounds open a space for us to find
The life we deeply desire.

The cure for pain is in the pain.
The wound is the place where the Light enters you.

The Opening of Eyes

That day I saw beneath dark clouds,
the passing light over the water
and I heard the voice of the world speak out,
I knew then, as I had before
life is no passing memory of what has been
nor the remaining pages in a great book
waiting to be read.

It is the opening of eyes long closed.
It is the vision of far off things
seen for the silence they hold.
It is the heart after years
of secret
conversing,
speaking out loud in the clear air.

It is Moses in the desert
fallen to his knees before the lit bush.
It is the man throwing away his shoes
as if to enter heaven
and finding himself astonished,
opened at last,
fallen in love with solid ground.
                    —David Whyte

Our home can be our safe space on solid ground
Where we open
And set free the river of our heart —

Our water, the silence it holds,

Astonished to find our Home there.
Our heart can break loose on the wind —
The wind on the water, Spirit's ocean below,
Eternal sky above, and
We as a uniting membrane.

Astonished.
Grateful.
Joyful.
Peaceful.
Healing.
Grateful.
Happy.
Real.
Peaceful.

BOOK II

Ways Of Dwelling

Dwelling is moment-by-moment work — it's living into the fullness of each experience and letting Love express itself through us. We can't look outside our self for our Home — we create our own ways of Dwelling. The following ways, then, are offered as a candle — a small beacon of light, enough for you to find your own windows to gather Light and Love.

For the vision explored here, there are two ways of Dwelling —
> Dwelling Within Ourselves, by entering Images of Home (inner space).
> Dwelling in Our World, by engaging with our home and place (outer space).

Each way is real. We can co-create the world in love with our inner responses, and our actions in the world, by paying attention to the images that come to us.

> **Listen to the presences inside poems.**
> **Let them take you where they will.**
> **Follow these private hints**
> **and never leave the premises.**
>
> **I am so small, I can barely be seen**
> **How can this great Love be inside me?**
> **Look at your eyes, they're small**
> **but they see enormous things.**
>
> **Walk to the well.**
> **Turn as the earth and the moon turn**
> **circling what they love.**
> **Whatever circles, comes from the center.**
> > **– Rumi**

A FEW WORDS ON IMAGES

An image is a message from spiritual realms, and can take any form — from a fall leaf, falling right in front of us, giving us a color palette for a painting we're working on; to an internal insight, a clue for resolving an unresolved issue.

An Image is a life-giving impulse — the presence inside poems — of the ineffable Love-energy that is the heartbeat of the cosmos. An Image embodies logos, holds a sliver of divine intelligence. An Image is the luminosity of the moon, a reflection of the unfathomable splendor of Love. We may have small eyes, but we have the capacity to see and experience enormous things.

Images are within us, lying as pearls, buried in dreams, memories, ancestry and our inner knowing; and, all around us, as constellations in the night sky. Images lie waiting for us to find amongst the leaves of a forest floor, or they can burst into our knowing, as a comet. However they come to us, they are helpers illuminating our path. Images are seeds given for us to plant and work with, to bring to life in worldly form, as inspiration.

Images can come to us in any form and through any sense — they can be held in a gesture, color, an inner impulse, a way of being. Our experience of the world is played out on a stage where everything is a part of our story — everything is purposeful — and we are a part of everything's story. Dwelling is our way to give form to the voices in our story.

An Image embodies a spark — it is Spirit's Light — of Union with Spirit. We look all around for THE answer, yet Love's touch is all around us in each breath we take. We long for bursts of enlightenment, yet Love grows slowly within us, through the waves of Spirit that shape the bordering shore we are. Dwelling through the gentle rhythm of receiving Images forms the solid ground from which we can take in the 1000- volt emotional-tsunamis when they hit.

The beauty we love is brought to us in Images. Beauty isn't merely pretty —

pretty things are a tonic to our numbness, at best only soothing our pain. Beauty is what is truthful, has integrity, unites us at our core and leads us into the fullness of our humanity. Artists — which we all are — are touched by an Image, their expression of which awakens and inspires us.

(MEET)ING AN IMAGE

I am offering four ways to take in an Image — Meditating on, Entering, Engaging with, and Touching (MEETing). MEETing an Image is a way of experiencing and taking in — through our heart — its mysterious power, letting it become a part of us.

MEETing an Image involves letting go of our attachments and accepting what has been brought to us is a part of something greater than ourselves, and our path to growing into wholeness. Spirit changes every nano-second, as the clouds. So can we. Does a salmon egg know it's going to become a powerful fish, whose body refracts the sun's rays, and is an essential part of its ecosystem? No, it just grows into the light, and holds firm amidst whatever is brought to it. So can we.

We can begin MEETing an Image by opening to what it has to offer, let a part of it shimmer, calling our attention. We can sink into its voice, sit with it, in silence — hear what it's offering. Then give artistic expression to what we hear — we can reveal a facet of our Home, the union of our soul with the Image. When we MEET an image, we open a door for something to happen — for Love's touch. Once our free-flowing response runs its course, we can sit back and reflect on what has taken form. Don't think about it, feel into it; listen for what arises.

90

Then we can ask for guidance. How can the life-giving impulse we received be embodied and integrated into our life? What does the Image mean for us? How can we live with its loving presence?

Just like it isn't possible to know the flavor of an apple without trying it, it isn't possible to know the mystery of life by using the mind. The communion with the Eternal, the divine ecstasy, takes place at the level of the heart. It isn't possible to describe this experience in words. But through art, it is possible to have a small taste of an apple's flavor. Art brings us closer to the mystery.
— Sri Prem Baba

MEETing an Image can be verbal, written or oral, yet our connection sinks deeper when our response rises out of our depths, beyond thought. Artistic expression, bursts of creativity — drawing, painting, sculpting, dancing, playing music, singing your song — reach through our dense layer of reasoning.

The first act to singing our song — open (our mouth)! Take a deep breath and let flow out what comes. Do it again, singing louder. With each opening, Spirit will flow more fully. Never stop. This is true with all forms of expression.

And those who were seen dancing
Were thought to be insane
By those who could not hear the music.
— Nietzsche

Picture this — a man standing in a shallow stream, water swirling through his legs. On his arms and legs are a series of metal rings. He moves his body as a part of the stream's flow, with the rings rolling around, making music. This can be our life — to be in communion with our earth, our place, and make music!

What follows are a variety of ways to give expression to your unique experiences of Images of Home for Dwelling.

DWELLING WITHIN OUR SELF

MEET A CANDLE

Being with a candle is the most humble, direct way to Dwell. There is only us, and light — that's all it takes to expand into spiritual realms.

A candle can sanctify our daily living, it'll immediately transform a space. We can light a candle before going to bed, and sit with it until its presence calms us; put it next to our computer; center our dining table; bring calm to a difficult conversation.

Light a single candle. Sit still. Gaze at the candle. Feel it transform the space. Listen for what it has to tell you. Do this before you read any further; it'll help the images sink in deeper.

OPEN YOUR HEART

I have a friend who, when she listens to you, does so with her whole heart. You can see her heart in her eyes, beaming love; nothing clouds the connection.

Many experiences can open our heart, such as listening to music, being in nature, seeing a hurt dog, making love. Yet, it's primarily through life's constant vigorous rubbing that our heart slowly opens as the rising sun, each moment further illuminating our world. Slowly, we develop compassion and a sense of charity.

We can also, in the moment, focus on opening our heart. Consider when suddenly finding yourself in a difficult conversation — soften into your heart, and open to the other. The space that unites you can be cleared, which will then open both of your hearts. Peace enters through open hearts.

SEE THROUGH MENTAL CONSTRUCTS
What you really see/ You are that.

The moon is always full — it's our perception that is limited. Spirit's Light is always with us — it's our mental constructs that blind our knowing this. Life is limitless, yet we contain ourselves in fear-cages and fall under the spell of this world's illusions. Everything is a mental construct, other than our bodies, the earth and the stars. These constructs are a dense fog blinding us from our true reality. Art transcends false mental constructs, slowly building firm ground amidst shifting tides. Our work is to stand on solid ground, plant ourselves there, and grow through the fog to the Light through the art of our living.

Our deeper presence is formless, one with our Source — we're a drop in the Love-ocean, we're a ray of Spirit. We can live with this awareness, and see and listen without judgment or thought. We can receive a person, plant, dog — all beings — and enter the space that unites us. We further root our self through each uniting space; we expand our self into each space we enter, and open our connection to Spirit.

MEET "THERE IS SOME KISS WE WANT," AND "THE SWAN"

Spirit beckons us to bring forth our deeper presence through the spaces we're in — in our heart, home and earth.

We can consider our soul as a home. There are many rooms, some in the light of Love, and some closed off through the sorrows and separations of one's life — they are too painful to re-enter. Dwelling encloses a safe space where we know we are held in Love, enabling us to open our closed-off spaces, and bring light to these disconnected parts of ourselves. Dwelling is our way to rediscover our pearl — our luminous core — and see we are amidst a loving body of seawater that is begging us, and helping us, bring forth and live through our pearl.

MEET your pearl, explore its luminosity. What parts of you are being embraced? What do you see through your love-window? What do you experience when the moon breathes into you? What do you want with your whole life?

Also, consider "The Swan." What is your water, your life-giving elements and forces? One element could be water, which can take form in your home as a fountain, the sound of which centers your home in a peaceful vibration; or blue flowing translucent curtains, luminous, creating waves of light and shade; or rooms with curving walls, flowing one into another.

Further, what spaces do you glide elegantly in, where you know yourself? These are mirrors of your Self.

MEET "LET THE BEAUTY YOU LOVE BE WHAT YOU DO"

This poem addresses the constant harsh truth of existence — we are empty, and life is frightening. Accepting our human condition is our first and most important step to finding our real way to truth and peace and wholeness — filling our emptiness. Dwelling is a way to break free of the numb imprisonment of our denial.

To be rich is to not want — our path is as simple as humbly letting the beauty we love be what we do. We access our beauty in hundreds of ways — consecrated, intentional actions; kisses — with the ground, the earth, our source of all life.

Play your soul-musical instruments — ways to engage with the world through your heart. Play music, or whittle, or garden, or paint, or write poetry, or swim in the ocean, or go for a walk in the woods, or contemplate a work of art, or sing. Our voice is the first musical instrument. Singing is the sound of the angels, revealing Spirit. Singing lifts up an experience, fills and sanctifies a space, as a candle. Carrying a song or hymn within us throughout the day, perhaps occasionally singing or whistling a verse, keeps us in Spirit's ocean.

MEET A BODY PRAYER AS AN EXPERIENCE OF THE CRUCIBLE OF HOME

The dynamics of this prayer opens us to experience our body — and, home, as they are one — as life-giving and absorbing vessels. This body prayer creates a heart-opening into Spirit, our place and companions.

Stand still with closed eyes, feeling the firm earth beneath you, body at rest. Imagine yourself as a tree with roots extending into the source that nurtures you while lifting up into the sky. Imagine yourself as a crucible, reaching out to the earth and all life, all suffering and joy. The center, your heart, is your place to receive and give love.

Breathe in the life you desire, exhale the disease you are growing through.

Ask for communion with all that you behold, and protection from anything not integral to your life. Ask to further open your heart to the love all around you.

Slowly, effortlessly, let your arms lift straight up to the sky while firming yourself into the earth. As you reach your limit upwards, feel the flow of the earth meeting the sky's energy in your spine. Feel the fullness in your heart. Feel the energy unleash in your spine and give you strength.

Let your arms slowly come down by the weight of all that you're receiving. As your arms come near your head, let them extend out to the horizon. Reach out to your relationships. Listen for which ones come up. Hold these.

Slowly sweep your arms in front, across the arc of your world, drawing those relations into your center by bringing your hands to your heart. Hold still and feel the swell of the love in your life, and the cavity of sorrow. Bring these to Spirit's Light, which resides in your heart.

Once settled, let your arms extend out in front of you, to give away the Love that you are. See the full extent of the garden of your life. Let your arms fall to your sides. Offer gratitude for your place in the world.

Make a clay sculpture expressing your experience of this exploration.

MEET YIN-YANG IMAGES OF HOME

A beauty of our human condition is that both sides of the paradox are true — we're meek, small creatures, and we are huge fish in the Love-ocean. The sparks that ignite from this dynamic are what keep us alive and growing. False comfort denies this reality; true peace resides in our Middle Way.

What is your life's expression of the Middle Way for each polarity. Each pole is a wing of the spiritual bird you are, flying Home.

Our home is an expression of our polarity-dance — we're fluidly moving in each polarity's spectrum. Or we're stuck in one place, as when standing in the sand, being slowly destabilized us as each wave — Spirit's offering — returns to the ocean. Perhaps we're now feeling stronger, after a trying time, so we're wanting expansive spaces for our healing to grow into; or we're drawn to soft, curvy spaces, as we've been connecting with the earth after finishing graduate school.

MEET YOUR MANY SELVES

We are constellations of selves — multiple stars forming a whole, united in infinity. Each star — self — holds a life-force. We have an ambitious self, a creative self, a sloth self, a solitude-seeking self, a gregarious self…

Each self is vital, and needs space to express itself. Consider a self at a time – MEET it and let it speak. Each exploration will reveal what each self desires.

Our many selves can be met in small intimate places within our home and through interaction with the larger world outside of our home. A window seat with a view of a favorite part of our garden can give our introverted self the silence needed to begin our day with a clear mind. Painting a wall in our dining room a luscious color can spark our sensual self. Having a favorite coffee house where we meet friends expands our home — and our extroverted self — into our urban fabric. Our nature-self can be met by listening to the birds as they awaken with us — recognizing their calls and considering their migrations and the distant places into which they weave our existence.

Some of our selves — our unresolved parts — reside in the lower realms of our self. Our disconnected selves need a space to express their self, to clear their self, which is their path to healing.

MEET YOUR CHILD

When you were a child, what did you like to do most? What did you want to be when you grew up? Who were the people you admired? Who were your heroes? These are signs or coordinates that show us the path to be walked in this life. A child arrives in this world with the memory of its soul's purpose. Eventually, due to external influences such as beliefs and social or cultural patterns, the child constructs a false sense of self and begins to disconnect from its essence. As a result, the child forgets about these first clues that were directing it towards what he or she came to do.

— Sri Prem Baba

Further, what spaces were you drawn to as a child? Did you like to (a) burrow into the earth, or (b) be up in a tree house? (c) swim in the ocean, (d) or tend to a campfire? These spaces are secure footholds, offer inner peace, that opens us into who we are.

The life-giving impulses within each experience can be embodied into your existing home. Same order as previous paragraph — your home could have (a) a room nestled within the interior of your home, with one small window, and wood paneling; (b) or a high space overlooking the woods, with just enough enclosure to make it safe while also a part of the woods; (c) or a room with an expansive view, full of glass — glass is water rendered still — and light; (d) or a centering hearth.

Continue this exploration — what spaces have you been drawn to in other parts of your life? How have those places corresponded to your psychic state, such as, when depressed, wanting inward, darker spaces?

You can record these spaces for your children.

ENGAGE WITH AND AWAKEN THE SOFT ANIMAL OF YOUR BODY

What does your most earthly, sensual self love?

To be a dog!? Rolling in the mud, a pile of leaves, the grass. Perhaps to tumble down a hill, or jump up and down — feel the wind's spirit, the solid earth, gravity's pull. Try burying yourself in the sand, or the earth — dirt is real, and good!

Stand tall into the wind — let it flow through you, and move with it.
Play in the surf, be rolled by a wave — feel the ocean's life force flow through you. After body surfing all day, I feel the ocean flow through me all night.

MEET YOUR "SELF-PORTRAIT"

Express your self-portrait — an honest expression of who you are. Look lovingly at your life, without judgment or blame. Healing is only possible when we bring, and give, our whole self to Spirit's Light. Consider each of the following questions —
*   Where do you feel loved?
*   Where do you feel betrayed?
*   Where do you feel safe and secure?
*   Where do you feel vulnerable?
*   What is truly supportive in your life?
*   What do you deeply know and feel connected to?
*   Where do you belong, and where do you feel abandoned?
*   Do you know despair?
*   Are you prepared to live in the world with its harsh need to change you?

What are your questions? Don't worry about answers. Life's unfolding is a process of living into our questions. It's enough to clearly state our questions. Our questions form the steps in our journey, and as a question's answer begins to appear, another question arises for us to reach towards.

All of our questions sprout from these seed-questions — Who am I? Where am I from? Where am I going? These work together in a triple-helix — they cross-pollinate and expand each other; they form the dynamic of our continual spiral journey towards our center.

Often the questions are two-sided, asking us to find their Middle Way. Our questions do not have right or wrong answers.

Sometimes our answers burst forth, sometimes they are so subtle that we barely notice them becoming a part of us.

Our questions are fuel for our fire. Our questions are reverberations from our longings. We move along our path by living into our longings.

We can embrace our answers when we look back/ with firm eyes/ saying this is where I stand. We stand in our home — Here I am! Our questions are summer breezes, filling and flowing through our home and Home. An answer appears as when first noticing the scent of a flower — that's a rose! — that then becomes a part of us. Our home and Home then take clearer form — perhaps we wake up a bit less agitated, even peaceful, as does our home feel; our old, wood dining table may seem to have more warmth; or the streaming light into our home appears more radiant, as is our heart.

You can also reveal your questions by exploring Images that intrigue you — that appear in your daily living — although you don't know why. Images are Love-notes from our spiritual friends — what are they offering? Rest in silence with your friend — sit, open your heart, and listen. If nothing appears, carry the question with you until an answer comes through, when the inner clouds are dissolved by Spirit's Light.

MEET THE CHALICE OF YOUR BODY

Our bodies are crystal clear vessels, like a baby's eyes, channels for Love's Light.

But life takes its toll on our bodies. Everything that happens around us — stress from too much work, environmental destruction, angst from our litany of oppression and suffering — leaves an imprint in our body. One way to consider illness is it didn't just arise out of our body. Many of our physical ailments are spiritual at core — a spiritual energy rode in the wave of our world physically bombarding us, and embedded into our body, which generated a physical component.

With closed eyes, scan your internal body. Notice any places where energy is blocked, or muscle tightness, or sore joints. These may not be us — they can be unclean spiritual energies living in us. While most of us have developed chronic symptoms requiring extensive physical healing, we can begin to unleash these energies.

MEET them, one at a time. Connect with and call in your Light-channel, your unique link between the earth and sky, which you can open via the body prayer, or yoga, etc. Offer this light-path to your unwanted guest; bless it on its journey to our source.

Although you may not feel different — subtle energies take time to feel a noticeable impact — you will begin healing in your body. As your home mirrors your bodies' well-being — they are one — you'll begin to notice your home feeling clearer. Further, your inner healing will ripple throughout all of existence — including the dark spiritual forces that caused your suffering.

Conversely, cleaning your home will make you feel better. All seemingly mundane home chores — done with mindfulness — create openings for Spirit to fill us. This dynamic can be extrapolated into endless actions — opening a window on a bright, fresh spring morning opens us to take into our hearts the scent of the flowers and the bird's calls; polishing a piece of furniture warms our blood; gardening nurtures the earth, and cultivates our senses; lying down to sleep at night returns us to our earth mother, into her womb, from where we travel into Spirit.

MEET VISUAL IMAGES OF HOME

MEET a provocative visual Image that has been with you for years, or suddenly appears. Work with the Image as when considering a dream — Images hold layers of information. Consider yourself as all characters in the Image — people, trees, clouds, buildings; all of it. Consider every aspect of the Image as sacred, as embodying a ray of our great loving mystery.

Consider the photograph titled, "Minimata," by W. Eugene Smith, of the mother and child in a bath. It's a modern Pieta. We all carry the pain of this child within us. We can't respond fully to our ecological crisis — the child was born with severe physical defects due to industrial contaminants in the mother's drinking water while she was pregnant — until we internalize the devastation of the earth, and our suffering.

DWELLING IN OUR WORLD

We are nature. Anything we create when we're humble — true to our nature — and centered in our heart nurtures us, connects us to our source, and feeds our larger world.

Over time, we imbue a place with soul — witness ancient sacred sites, or old, worn homes. Our lives are deepened as we open to and ask for the presence such a place holds. Spirit feeds us regardless, yet, the more deeply we MEET our home and place, the more we take hold of the power held within.

Dwelling reaches deepest with unprocessed nature — the farther an element is removed from its natural state, the less it nurtures us — yet, that doesn't mean we have to live in the wilderness. We can do this work in the city — we can Dwell in a prison cell — although nothing can equal the power of a primal forest.

If we don't let the natural world live into its full life, our ability to commune with its life potency is weakened. What is there to do, given the enormity of our ecological crisis? Praise and love everything. Let everything live the life it was born to live. Be a co-creative part of everything's unfurling. Don't see nature as a resource to fuel our self-serving ways, to devour and make money off. Build the world in Love, one home at a time.

DEVELOPING AWARENESS OF LIFE ALL AROUND US

OPEN UP TO AND BREATHE IN THE BEAUTY AND POWER OF NATURE

Our simple, heart-centered interactions with nature — think St. Francis and his pure love for all things and beings — restore the earth as they heal us. When we so engage, a door opens for Spirit to work through us. All of creation, and divine beings, are waiting for us to ask them to commune with us.

I spent my twenties driving back and forth from Santa Barbara to Washington, DC, looking for my place. During each trip, I spent a lot of time in the southwest. I was quite unconscious, yet some force in that otherworldly terrain began waking me up. Something began stirring. Is there a place that so speaks to you?

A somewhat different experience — once, when in a difficult transition, feeling lost, I sat on a rock in the middle of a stream. The gently passing water was soothing, and then a hummingbird came right up to me. I could have touched him. He stayed with me for a while, making sure I got his message — all is well. Has a messenger come to you? Can you reflect and now see when you had a visit from such a friend?

Know that Spirit is the shine of the sun, moon and stars, and is in the wind — we are always swimming in Spirit's ocean. We are children of the Great Love — we're made of the same particles found throughout the cosmos, charged with the same power.

There are hundreds of ways to kneel and kiss the ground. Here are a few —
Take in deeply an experience, such as a meal — do nothing else, just eat. Taste all flavors, be mindful of where each ingredient came from, the work and love involved to bring it to you; or observe deeply a flower, notice the world it creates, the universe at its center; or the play of shadows on a wall from a tree in the wind.

Observe the play of light on forms. Engage with light, the sun's rays, moving across deep space to illuminate our world. The sun's light only knows itself as it meets matter. In anything we see, we co-create the world with our Source — from the sun's rays bouncing off the object, into our eyes, charging every cell. At the same time, something in us reaches out to meet the light — the spark from this meeting creates a space that unites us with the light. Mirroring the sun's light, Love travels on the vibrations of Light. We're always being filled with Love.

Engage with the moon, take in its majesty. Behold the geometry and immensity of the space between its companions, the earth and sun. Take in the moon light — light coming from the sun, bouncing off the moon, diffusing into mystery as it meets our heart — Breathe into me! Consider how the moon controls life on earth.

Enjoy — be in joy with — the play of elemental forces of nature on earthly form — water and wind's affect; the aging and decomposition of all living matter, returning to their source, becoming food for the next wave of life; rising bubbles in a glass of sparkling water; the vibrancy of rain falling on a still pool; the wind sashaying through the trees.

Observe a rose. Empty your mind, open your inner knowing, and see the inner presence of the rose. See it for itself, not your projections. Attempt to take in the world this way as you walk through your day.

Consider a piece of fruit. It's sunlit-colored water, formed as it drew out nutrients from its sources — the earth through a tree, and the sun — and alchemically became nectar juice. So are we.

There is also an element's inner presence — vibration — it emits, and the dynamics of its motion. Consider water, our essential source of sustenance, vitality, rejuvenation, and cleansing. There are many mysteries water reveals when MEETing it, as is true for all elements.

Go deep into wilderness. Unplug from your daily living. Breathe in the deep life-force. Be filled with nature's vibrations, not those from the roar of machines and hum of our electronic gadgets.

Engage with a tree, our primal companion — form a relationship. Consider it as an expression of your life: How it stands, with roots reaching deep and far for sustenance and community — tree roots intertwine, forming a network of gathering — with trunk and limbs reaching to the sky; how the light draws it out of its safe womb of soil; how it stands, strong yet vulnerable to the forces that nurture it, and rip off its limbs. Consider the community of creatures that live in its realm.

Make nature art, such as pioneered by Andy Goldsworthy. Find an intimate nook in your place, see it as a canvas to heighten poetically. Feel into the place, see if anything is calling you. Perhaps you're drawn to the base of a tree, and work with leaves to create a portal (for Alice in Wonderland!); or, link twigs in a spiral, flowing from a branch; or, make a spirit home, nestled into some rocks.

Notice and feel weather changes — how when a front moves in, all matters of life transform. Know how a weather system rolls down from Canada, or up from the Gulf of Mexico — the weather weaves many of us together. Try standing, facing into a cold winter wind — let Canada chill, and enliven you.

ATTUNE WITH NATURE'S RHYTHMS

The heartbeat of nature is her steady pulse — the rhythm of the earth. We too need rhythm in our daily living, to be open to what is already beating in us.

Consider this — our heart doesn't pump. It gives our blood, our juice, with its own life-force, a rest, a pause, before it makes its life-giving journey through our body. This is our ocean's waves moving through us, with each retracting wave being a pause. This is the genesis of our bodies' rhythm, of flow and rest, yin and yang.

Engage with the turning of the Earth. The earth is always turning, towards its source, the sun. Whatever circles, comes from the center — the spirit world is always inviting us in. This is an overarching way we're innately pulled into union with our source. Feel this deep in your body; visualize this cosmic picture.

Find a place in nature where you feel a loving presence. Be still. Let the natural world's pond of motion resettle from your arrival. Listen for nearby presences; take it all in. Soften your gaze. Pay attention to your breathing, which will begin to attune to the rhythm of the place. Over time, you become a part of the place.

Experience each day holding a rhythm of hope — sunrise — and the uncertainty of darkness — sunset. Each day is a microcosm of our life — the freshness, quietness, softness, gentleness of sunrise; the calm closure, pause for reflection, threshold of the mystery of darkness; all completed by the deep night, a type of death, to be reborn in the morning.

Know your waters — the creek in your neighborhood feeds into a river, which feeds into the ocean. Then that same water evaporates, and returns as rain on your garden. That is the flow of life. Our life follows a similar sequence.

Know when the trees lose their leaves, the flowers rise up in Spring — what is the first sign of Spring? Know where to greet each rising flower, and remember their home all year. Praise them — a flower's center mirrors the cosmos.

Observe all of the life around you, the players on your stage. Notice when the birds awaken, the screech owl hoots, the raccoons come out, the bees light on the flowers... they all have a rhythm.

Let your body fall into natural rhythms. All of our activities need rhythm — when we eat, exercise, sleep. As a bear, sleep more in winter. Our sleep life is as active as our waking hours — our dreams are as real as our experiences in the world.

Enjoy the sensuality — awakened, emotionally vibrant and responsive body — of each season. During winter, we can sit by a fire; make soup and tea; go out and get very cold, and then burrow into the warmth of our home; or find a protected place, out of the wind, and let the sun reach deep into our body.

Plant and tend a garden. This is perhaps the most direct way to be rooted into the earth, and be a part of Her cycles.

Be aware of the sources of your sustenance, know their life-cycles. Eat what is grown in your region, seasonally; or at least be aware of the consequences of your choices.

Develop orientation in the world, be as a sundial. Know where the four cardinal points are, where the sun sets and rises — this is another central rhythm. Observe where the breezes come from and notice how their rhythm is to pick up after the sun has warmed the earth — thermals rise up and slowly accumulate into rising wind. As the sun warms the earth's waters, evaporation rises into clouds. Notice how the winter winds and summer breezes come from different directions, creating their own rhythm of keeping earthly matter in motion and vitalized.

DWELLING THROUGH YOUR HOME AND PLACE

Develop intimacy with, and engage with, the home and place you behold – learn what it responds to and what parts of it resonate for, and enliven, you.

By refracting through the crystal of our heart, we expand spiritual Light into our world. And we know our world through the sun's light. Dwelling creates openings for both lights, and unites these lights. Our Home is Light — as spiritual beings, we are formless pure Light. Our home captures the sun's light, and creates shade and shadow. Shadow is silence, which allows us to know Light, and balances light. This communion is the life-line for Dwelling in our home.

We came to the earth to build our spiritual Home, in part, through Dwelling. As we come to know our Home, it incarnates in us, and in our home. We are one being. Creating my home was my big-bang — all matter of thought formed into my constellation, my knowing of Home through making my home.

Consecrate your home — our greatest act of co-creation, which comes forth when humbly being aligned in Spirit, is conceiving and birthing a child. Every action can be so consecrated. With every breath, every act, we can bring spirit's Light and Love into our world. The following ways of Dwelling consecrate our life as we live in our home.

OUR HOME CAN BE A PLACE OF REFUGE

Our home's spaces and walls can resonate repose, opening us to peace and truth and beauty; permanence, substance, simplicity, joy, balance, humility, authenticity, tradition/ancestry. You can embody such impulses as you engage in the making of your home.

These impulse's presence are formed from nature — spaces filled with light and sound and color which give life to walls made of real materials with scale, proportion, rhythm, form, and texture attuned to our deepest human impulses.

Each space and surface of our home provides an opportunity to make a gesture towards the natural world, and is a way of uniting our home with our place. Our home is a vessel, uniting us with our place.

Building forms can be sensual and alive, as our body, not rigid and hard and lifeless. Surfaces can have vitality, hold an intention attuned to what we want to experience in each room — be soft, or vibrant, or rough, or glassy/reflective, etc. You can vitalize a wall by putting your attention towards it, by engaging with it. Consider a glazing paint, such as Lazure, which makes drywall luminous, and redeems it; or a deep, rich color, vibrant as the activity in that room (further, you can paint your intention for each room in words first, in the same color, then paint over them); or a thin coat of plaster, such as American Clay; or wood; or fabric.

Feel the firmness of the floor, the comfort of each wall you press against. Feel the expansion and connection of each window, the anticipation and fear of each door, the sheltering of each ceiling.

The spaces of our home can hold ancient spatial archetypes — of space, form and sequences — from the natural world. We can go through dense woods (dark passageways), opening into pastures (rooms). The shape of a room can be other than efficient right-angled corners. Corners can be softened, chamfered, attuned to our bodies. Walls can have texture, rooms can vary in height. Light can be mysterious. We can recall when humans burrowed into the earth, via a dark, inward, secure, private room; or sprang across tree branches, via a light, tall, wood-framed hideaway.

ENGAGE WITH THE PLACE THAT EMBRACES YOUR HOME

Via Dwelling, you can expand your knowing of your Self out into the world, and beyond, throughout the cosmos.

In the way that our breath is perhaps our most vital aspect of living, our home can breathe, drawing in the world around us and expanding us out into our place. Spaces can reach out from the core to respond to places that call us — to gather daylight, pull in the ocean breezes, track the arc of the moon's journey, or the sound of the rain. And our home can expand out our awareness — connect us to a compelling view; orient us to a majestic tree; take us into the adjacent deep woods.

Just as we breathe in and out, one space can be expansive, while another space can be inward-focused, setting up a centrifugal and centripetal dynamic — with our heart at the center, drawing in and releasing out. Our home can provide place for inner, reflective solitude, and outward-reaching gatherings.

You can feather your home into its place, engage in the uniting membrane. You can define and occupy outdoor spaces to unite you with your place — sit on a porch during a storm; rest in shaded spaces to stay cool in the summer; set a fountain in an intimate garden just outside where you meditate.

Our home can be in the curl of a wave, which is the meeting of the deep energy of the ocean with our firm earth. Our home can also put us in-between realms — our home can be just inside the edge of a forest overlooking a meadow, or we can sit in a bay window overlooking a city street. Such experiences give a vibrancy to our living and open up reflective chords.

Mirror spatial experiences in your place in the making of your home. A curving edge of a table can mirror the rolling hills beyond; a flat prairie can be mirrored by a canti-levering, flat ceiling (think Frank Lloyd Wright); a dappled forest can be mirrored by a vine-covered patio trellis.

Observe the wind as it moves across the canopy of trees overhead, listen to the song it plays, and take in the vitality of its breath passing through your home and body.

Open curtains and welcome each new day, our daily re-beginning. Greet the sun and be grateful for its nurturing and power. Be grateful for our secure refuge amidst the terror of the world. There is no greater sense of Home than a single candlelit cabin with a small fire, alone amidst deep wilderness in a raging storm.

The train that rumbles by, or the plane above, are reminders that we live in a world-wide-web of civilization, weaving and flowing together, and that most of us are working together to make a better world.

ENGAGE WITH YOUR HOME AS A SAILBOAT

Pay attention to, and engage with, your home as a vessel that can put you in more intimate relationship with the world around you.

Observe the prevailing winds, where storms come from, the arc of the moon and sun. Your home can respond to — open to, or be protected from — these forces, and be in relationship with them.

Invite nature's voice in — put up sundials to be in dialogue with the sun; weathervanes and chimes to dance and sing with the wind; flags to show the flow of the wind; plantings to encourage native habitat, and feed migrating birds; bird feeders and baths to invite this most precious, song-full companion.

Read and know your home as a watch — know when the sunlight warms up each room, observe how the quality of light at dawn changes throughout the year. As our home is our second layer of enclosure beyond our body, you are really observing how you meet your place.

Live in your home as a sundial — breakfast room receives morning light; your study absorbs the afternoon light; your dining room basks in the sunset, vibrant as the food you receive.

Quality of light in each room responds to use of the space and its relationship to its contiguous exterior space, creating a tapestry of light and dark.

Be a cat — occupy sunny spaces in the winter, and live closer to the center (hearth); in the summer, rest in shady spaces, live on the periphery, live outdoors.

Light fires in winter — the hearth (heart of your home) is then your center of living. In the summer, your hearth may be a pond with a waterfall; or multiple hearths — centers of life — in the gardens orbiting around the inward hearth.

Open windows for air, the sound of the rain, and for ventilation.

Put window shades up and down, responding to the sun's movement.

Chop wood, carry water. Most of us now have resources pumped into our homes, but you can be aware of how your home is conditioned, where your water comes from, where your waste goes. And you can lessen your impact — harvest rainwater for gardening, turn the heat down and wear sweaters.
Landscaping can cool your home in summer, let the sunshine in during winter.

Let interior air temperature be relative to the exterior temperature. Our body needs to expand and contract with the seasons. Avoid a hermetically sealed home at a constant 70°.

Enjoy simple, enlivening pleasures amidst our complex world. Consider chores as mindful practice — the Zen of sweeping! Keep your home's vibration peaceful — limit vacuums and other household machines. Hang your clothes to dry, watch the flow of the wind through your sheets. Place fragrant plants nearby for your clothes to hold their scent — you then sleep in the flower's charm.

ANIMATE SPACE

Each space is begging us to break open and become further alive. Each space offers ways to know more fully our Self, and the place we behold.

We can engage with the spaces of our home by creating imaginative associations — live as children! Each space elicits a response that helps us give expression to our psychic condition — what is present in our heart.

Consider a flight of stairs in your home. Stairs aren't simply a way to go up or down — they're a stage, beckoning us to bring forth and give expression to the specific moment in our life's journey. Do we bounce up, springing two steps at a time, hurling ourselves with tremendous pulls and pushes on the railing, giving sail to the wind of some exhalation? Or perhaps we glide down, with our feet pouring over the steps, lost within the flow of inner peace with our hand caressing the railing as an arm of a loved one we're thinking about.

Unleash the hidden presences in your life and home; give name and story to the elements and life-forces, and your relationship with them. Imagine the secret lives of all the characters that make your world. Take the sun — make a story that explains its origins and its relationship with you. Ancient civilizations created mythologies to explain the origins, workings, and their relationship to, the natural world. Then the scientific age wiped them out, and this aspect of our consciousness.

Music is liquid Architecture. Architecture is frozen music (Goethe). This is syntactical, and more deeply, lyrical. Space can be fluid; and form is still, seemingly, but its resonance can be vibrant. And we can consider our home as a musical instrument, that we play as we engage in our relationships in our home. We can also call forth our home's silent song with music — chant, drum, whistle — we can let the song of our heart's union with our home arise.

You can poetically create life-giving experiences from that which seems obtrusive, such as you can entertain that traffic noise as the ocean waves. Taking out smelly compost engages us with the cycle of preparing the soil, planting, gathering, preparing, eating, absorbing, and discarding. That smell is a door into experiencing an expansive life.

Energetically and vibrationally, the world is a Van Gogh painting. His illness opened him to see the life-force that lies hidden within everything. Soften your gaze, open your heart, look deeply into a landscape, and see what unfastens.

ENGAGE IN INTUITIVE FENG SHUI

All layers of our soul — body, home, and earth — have energy pathways and nodes. Our body's energy can be accessed via acupuncture, and our home and earth can be engaged with feng shui. We can develop the capacity to be in dialogue with the subtle energies and rhythms of the earth and stars as they weave through us and our home. We can learn to engage with and take hold of our inherent Union. There is no separation between you and the world and cosmos around you — acting in one realm is acting in the others. We change as the world around us does, and the world changes through what we hold and project. Just as you learn to respond to all parts of your self — body, mind, spirit — so can you learn to be intimately attuned to these life-forces.

As with gardening, the first act is to prune dead-matter, create openings for new life. Feel into each room and remove anything that doesn't resonate.

Locate yourself in a room in your home, sit still, clear your mind, and ask to be attuned with subtle energies. Listen. Slowly these life-forces begin to reveal themselves — you'll learn to see/feel invisible forces, and notice what is no longer life-giving.

Respond to what you hear, make a return gesture, co-create — move furniture, paint a wall, add a window, plant a tree, clean the room.

LIVE INTO PARADOX

Elements in dialogue, with that which balances them, create life-force.

Space can put us in the dynamics of paradox, perhaps by: An intimate bay window, perched out into the world, with an expansive view; a room can have dense and earthen walls and floor, with a light-filled, airy ceiling/roof; our home can offer protection, be nestled into the forest with firm walls, and pop up via a soaring, light-filled study; a primary wall can be of stone, with finely detailed wood cabinets floating on it; or our home can have soft, curving walls, with a steel filigree ceiling/roof.

PAINT THE CANVAS-WALLS OF YOUR HOME WITH YOUR STORY

We remember through stories. Our home is ensouled over time — spaces and walls hold memories and tell our stories.

Surround yourself with Images that are nurturing and hold Love-energy — remnants from experiences, travels, ancestral artifacts. The walls of our home change and thicken, as does our life's story.

Real materials absorb the vibrations of our experiences — the crash from a fight, the roar of laughter, the scents from cooking — that they emit as they absorb others, creating a vibrant texture.

Welcome imperfections, the tenacious voice of reality pressing through. Embrace the wear and scars of time and experience — they record our story of becoming real.

Warning — avoid clutter, know when it's time to prune. If something is stale with no life-force, it isn't feeding you.

ENGAGE WITH REAL MATERIALS FROM YOUR PLACE

Real materials resonate a deep life-force. We can consider each natural element — water, soil, fire, air/wind, sun, wood, stone — and ask how we can consciously interact with it as we create and live in our homes.

Begin this process by thinking of materials as the food we eat: the more our food lived a healthy life — with no pesticides, hormones, etc.; wasn't processed with chemicals or non-organic additives, etc.; was grown under the sky and fed nurturing food; wasn't injected with harmful, toxic substances, to resist the forces of nature — the more it feeds and nurtures us, and gives meaning to their life. Being surrounded by real materials, simply rendered, surrounds us with a vibration or resonance humankind has always known.

Craft real materials — interact, dialogue, commune with material. Your expressions through craft form the words of the book of your home with which you tell your story.

Materialism — having things is okay, as long as we're in relationship with them. We can only have so much, otherwise we live in chaos — unintentional, disconnected relationship with ourselves and the world with which we live.

Nothing is inherently bad; it's our relationship with a thing that is of issue. Things have value as we engage with them. When being humble and heart-centered, our actions can open up a space for Spirit to enter.

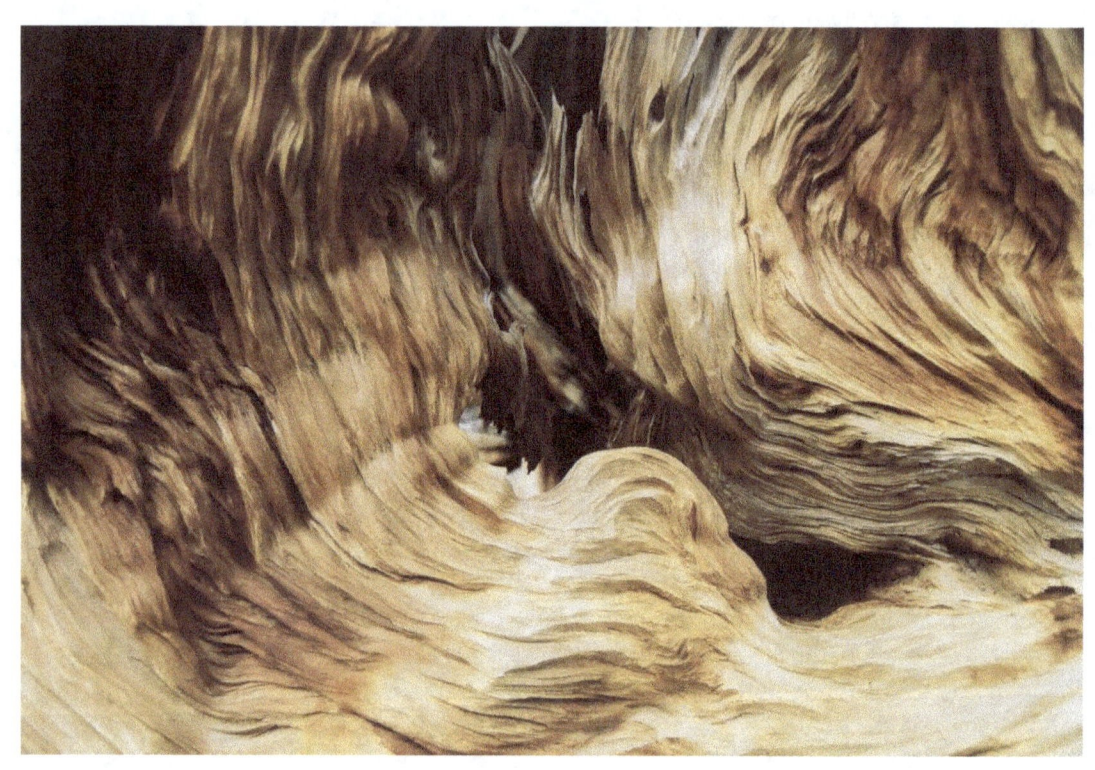

MEET THE PATTERNS IN "A PATTERN LANGUAGE"

This extraordinary book, by Christopher Alexander, explores 253 world-wide patterns of how we make and live in our home and place. Most of the patterns embody poetic aspects of Dwelling, and can help you further understand what Dwelling is offering regarding how you can make your home. Further, many patterns are embedded in the ways of dwelling in your home explored in Dwelling.

As you go through A Pattern Language, notice which patterns resonate. Reflect on why they speak to you, and consider how they can be doors for your Dwelling.

BOOK III

A Few More Ways Of Dwelling

The following writings expand and further ground Dwelling. The sun shines infinite rays of light — these writings are just a few rays, further illuminating more aspects of Dwelling.

A SPACE UNITES US

There is a space that unites two people — a luminous heart-space not of place or time. The core of our knowing of a loved one — our relationship — exists in this shared space. Even when they're not physically with us, this space holds us.

We are IN love — love is the name we give this space. We access this space through our heart.

This is true for all of our relationships, including our loved ones who have died and those alive who we don't see often. If we're open to this space, we can engage in this aspect of our relationships. Our love for our beloved is always alive — we can be with them regardless of where they are.

The pain and longing we feel for those departed or far away comes from our inner-union, as earthquakes rising from deep, shifting tectonic plates. Engaging in our heart-space doesn't take that pain away — our heart is complex and nuanced, capable of multiple ways of being.

What does all this mean? How can we be so engaged?

Being open to the possibility is the first step — belief is a door into unseen realms. Then learning to listen in a new way — when we're open to the ineffable, we create an opening for that world to make itself known. Both in silence and in those in-between moments — such as when lifting our head up from our work and walking to get a glass of water — our minds are clear to receive a sliver of understanding.

We are not this body — we are Love. Our deepest Self exists IN Love, in the relationships of our heart. This is the knowing that allows us to transcend most any condition we find ourselves in — we can endure most any pain or anguish over the illusions that surround us.

Living in our spirit-body doesn't mean we disregard our increasingly neutered and devastated planet. We can also be in Love with a tree or river or mountain — we can be open to their voice we hear in our silent uniting space. It's not important if they are sentient beings or have a beating heart. Recall living with the wonder of life with which a child sees the world — we can allow our imagination to experience and engage with the myriad of life forces swirling all around us. Our endless possible inner unions can expand us way beyond our small box of existence. This is our deeper ecosystem.

Our moment by moment choice — do I enter this space with the other?

Life can spring forth from these seeds of knowing Love. Watering these seeds — engaging with and nurturing all beings around us — happens freely when we open our heart to them.

THE FOUNDATION ON WHICH WE DWELL

A tree or our beautiful garden is not nature until it's integrated and understood as part of an ecosystem. While we have a natural world all around and within us, we are increasingly removed from the deeper rhythms and cycles and flow of our earthly source, and ourselves. We long ago ceased seeking harmony with nature — instead, we live as when riding a powerboat, moving as fast as we can with little consideration for the world around us. Here are a few ways we're as such disconnected; each is a simplification of complex issues for the sake of beginning a dialogue:

- We no longer cherish our earth, our home. Many of us live in environments that have been devastated by mindless development. If we don't live in the earth's beauty, how can we create with it?

- Many of us — and our children especially — spend little time outdoors, let alone in deep woods. We mostly live in the presence and sound of machines or glow of digital contraptions. We get in touch with nature through our screen savers and nature calendars; we seldom spend time in such places, listening to the animal calls and learning the names of the trees. The daily activities of the animals go unnoticed by us, and we fail to recognize our shared ways of living with the creatures roaming about.

- Humans have been born the same way since Day One, yet now many of us are born via C-sections, often for the sake of doctors' and hospitals' convenience. Many women are deprived of perhaps their most powerful, intrinsic, natural experience.

And our babies don't receive essential protective bacteria as they pass through the birth canal.

- Let's hope we're not what we eat — so much of our food is created in chemistry labs; our meat comes from animals that spend their lives in pens, fed inappropriately, drugged with hormones and "anti-biotics" — not an animal that has lived a full life. Partly because our bodies are no longer nourished by the foods created for us, we take many supplements and prescriptions — our bodies are medical experiments.

- Many buildings we find ourself in are sterile and highly ordered, rather than welcoming spaces and forms that breathe and resonate with our bodies and souls. Our homes are often a hermetically sealed capsule consuming vast quantities of energy to fend off the elements around us.

- We try to fight time with our fascination with youthful bodies and surface appearances, consuming face lifts and spa treatments and an endless array of cosmetics. Perhaps if we spent more time amidst the life cycles of nature, we'd approach aging without fear.

- We go to great expense to keep our ailing, aging loved ones alive — which in some cases causes their suffering — rather than let them pass on to their next place gracefully.

- We fly on planes — through the clouds, the setting sun, beholding the arc of the earth — with our window shades down, watching electronic screens.

This litany doesn't stop. What are we afraid of?

Our attachment to the material world that we've created, and our endless fascination with technological feats, are destroying the natural world — and thus ourselves — to serve our short-sighted aspirations.

Perhaps we are, at root, afraid of death, with no belief that there's something deeper of which we're a part. This has nothing to do with religion; rather it's a spiritual question. Or perhaps it's this: the world can be terrifying — it's not Eden — and thinking we need to exert and protect ourselves, rather than form synchronistic relationships, we maim the earth. Or, perhaps it's this:

> We are at the height of a profound planetary transformation that has been marked by a major environmental crisis. Within this context, the waters have been our greatest messenger. The waters of the world have shown us where we are on this evolutionary journey as well as the next steps that should be taken. Although many people are awakening as individuals, in collective terms, we are still very primitive. Our awareness is very low, so we do not hear the message that the waters have been trying to give us through droughts, storms, floods and tsunamis. Archetypally, the waters, like all of nature, represent the Universal Mother; which also includes our biological mother. What causes us to destroy nature and treat it as an object to be exploited? What happens when we don't see the spirit that inhabits all living beings? Behind this blindness lies a deep hatred for the mother.
> — Sri Prem Baba

Whatever is the mix underlying our condition, what is clear is we go to great lengths to separate ourselves from the natural world, yet we are another leaf on the great tree of life. We have created a sub-atmosphere of existence that has disengaged us from our earthly source. What is it we're becoming?

Is our condition bad, and are we in the process of a slow death?

No matter how confused we are about our evolutionary imperative, or whether we have one, what matters is up to us to reveal, with an open mind and body and soul, with all parts of ourselves engaged with the world around and within us. This is the true foundation upon which we Dwell. We can live in the city or a hut in the woods — our situation isn't important. What matters is our intention to revere and take our place within our ecosystem — in the relationships of our family and community and place. To name a few ways we can engage as such:

- We can wake up in the morning as our body tells us, open our eyes to the sky and changing leaves and birds on their early chores and ponder our own such goings on. We're all equal beings in our eco-system.

- We can enjoy our bodies' wisdom and yearnings — embrace our bodies' form; we are all beautiful — and listen to what it asks for rather than what our society tells us is good for us.

- We can look at the moon at night and expand our mind to seeing the moon's light-shape as result of the interplay of the sun and earth — the moonlight is the child of their interaction. And we can reflect on all the ways the moon influences life on earth.

- In creating our dwelling, we can provide security and refuge while being in open dialogue with the natural world.

- We can live in our homes as when sailing, where, through our engagement, we can be in intimate relationship with the world.
- We can reflect on the rivers which run through our lives, consider how they connect us to worlds up and down stream, how a myriad of life is given focus by those waters and shores. How is a network of rivers different than our city streets?

- We can sit in our garden, notice the wealth of life — plants and flowers and birds and bugs — and then look up and see the clouds unfurling, flowing from shape to shape. This is how we are held, with the gift of living in Spirit's garden.

- We can sit on our porch and notice how the robins fly to a decoy spot with a meal for their chicks, sit there observant of all life around, only to go to their nest when they know it's completely safe.

- We can plant a tree as part of our urban forest, as part of our surrounding woods, as part of what has planted itself for thousands of years in our ecosystem — to one day be food for future woodland-generations and for our great grandchildren's children to play under on a hot summer day.

- We can walk down a city street and watch the complex interplay of shades and shadows and reflections off glass buildings, feel the excitement of going down an urban "canyon" — all set into motion from our sun, very far away.

- When we fly, we can engage with where we are — seven miles up in the sky! How many thousands of years have humans looked up, seen the birds, wanting to be there? The atmosphere we're roaring through may have clouds worthy of a Dutch master painting. The earth reveals its endless colors and textures and patterns flowing every which way. And at night we can see iridescence, sparkling, glowing textures — and perhaps the rising moon.

- We can experience a loved one's death as a beautiful and profound experience — our greatest awakening and a way to surrender to nature's calling — rather than hiding their bodies in the bowels of a funeral home pickled with toxic chemicals.

The ways we can be more deeply engaged with worlds around and within us are boundless. All we need is found in nature, and in our imagination.

WE CAN VITALIZE AND BALANCE OUR LIFE THROUGH DWELLING

We can vitalize and balance our life by engaging, and forming relationship with that which has life-force. Our home is an organism that can breath and be in rhythm with the life-force of the earth and sky. Our home is our next layer of enclosure beyond our skin, and, as our skin, our home is an organ that is essential to our well-being. Our home can be healthful — feed our well-being — if we nurture it as we do our body. What follows are a few ways we can so consider, and live through, our home.

Our home is a vessel with exterior membrane-walls, forming a woven dialogue that can put us in relationship with our place. Further, our physical home and inner self mirror each other: As we live through our home, we give form to our soul; as we deepen our inner journey, we're more open to the world in which our home unites us. This dialogue is Dwelling.

Central to Dwelling is an awareness that we can live in our home as a sailboat. We tend to live in buildings as when riding a powerboat — we unconsciously flip on/off switches, triggering various mysterious machines, hermetically sealed from the natural world. We can live in our home as when sailing — we can pay attention to the wind and currents, adjust our home to respond to the flow of nature, engage with the ocean— breath the fresh air!

Our home can provide a place for the many selves that we are, giving us a balanced life. Our home can offer: expansive spaces that take us out of our self; intimate nooks where we can be inward and reflective; gathering spaces to be with friends and family; comforting rooms for when we're especially in need of healing; darker, inward spaces to retreat from the heat and hustle and bustle of life.

141

Nothing is more healing than being IN nature, and our home can put us in relationship with the natural world. This can happen spatially, as places in our home can be in intimate relationship with our garden, or a tree, or forest; capture summer breezes; provide sunny places to take in the earth's warmth; or track the arc of the sun and moon. We can also be connected to nature via the materials with which we build. Just as we want to eat food that is as close to its natural state as possible, as it holds more nutrients, so do we want to build with recognizable elements — earth, wood, stone — as they hold a deep resonance.

Relatedly, the uncomplicated act of tending a garden is perhaps the simplest yet effective way our living through our home can nurture us. This dialogue is completely reciprocal — as we tend our garden and reap a harvest, we can help to restore the earth.

Light! We are light, seeking light. Much of my work as an architect is cracking homes open to receive light, or designing new homes that act as a sundial, capturing light throughout the day, as appropriate to each room.

As with acupuncture, opening pathways in our home is vital to our well-being. The first act we can do in making our homes more healthful is to weed all clutter, prune all dead branches to make way for new life. And then we can intentionally arrange our home, aware of how it is a part of an energetic dialogue uniting all things, including the stars. We can engage with elements in our home, see them as living beings, not just inert, dust-collecting remnants of past lives.

Just as our body needs care and attention, so does our home. We tend to see maintenance or cleaning as a distraction from our busy lives. Alternatively, it may be seen as a respite, a working-meditation — a chance to get out of our heads. When we're feeling disconnected, afraid, lost, these simple, humble actions bring solace.

There is a lot of literature on healthy homes, much of which focuses on concerns such as non-toxic finishes and furnishings, and ventilating noxious fumes. All of that is important, but those don't get to the core issue. We receive the most healing when we work from the inside-out, which only comes through our conscious engagement. Rumi offers, *The pot drips what's in it.* The primary work is always a shift in awareness or consciousness. With fresh eyes — and an open heart — we can live in the world through our homes in a way that feeds and nurtures all parts of ourselves, our companions, and the earth.

SPACE CAN BE A PLACE FOR INTIMACY TO UNFOLD

Our home, and our knowing of Home, is not a discrete place — it is part of an ecosystem.

When our home feels lacking, in need of expansion or renewal, there are often more options than commonly understood. Before considering renovating or building, there are useful questions we can ask ourselves: Do we really need more space or things? How can we live more intentionally? What is it we are really looking for?

Perhaps the work at hand is within ourself.

Separating "needs" from "wants" is a part of our psychological and spiritual practice, and both the process of creating our home and living in our home can help us distinguish between these impulses. Exploring what Home means to us as an internal image can help us understand what is essential and life-giving, separated from the acquisitive trappings our society constantly throws at us. Our physical home can provide a still center of refuge where we find the silence in which clear thoughts are born.

Further, space can be a place for intimacy to unfold — nothing gives us a more profound sense of Home or Love than being met and heard in an intimate way. Space is the medium in which relationship is formed, whether it's in our heart or in our home. Slowly, through our connection to and engagement with the relationships of our family and community and place — all of which comprise our ecosystem — we move towards wholeness; we know our Home.

Yet too often space is just another commodity, another way to proclaim self- worth as measured in quantity or ostentatiousness. Where does that get us? Many homes have large rooms where families communicate with each other via email or texting, with no place to cuddle with a loved one or curl up and enjoy a quiet moment of reflection. And the spaces of our homes are typically internally oriented and cut off from the land — focused on a TV or computer screen — or they command a view rather than breathing in and out with the land, and being inextricably woven into a whole.

If we can understand our self to be as a part of a larger whole, we may feel less of a need to attempt to create an exclusive, discrete entity. Who needs a large home when we can engage in intimate relationships?

Often the work that needs to happen is internal, not external; in ourselves, not our shelters. If we take the time and use our imagination, we can engage in a dialogue between our Home and our home. They feed and teach one another, and each is always completed within a larger order or system or universe. Our home is the ocean surface, a painter's canvas telling the story of our soul-deep-waters meeting the luminous skies. Each realm engages with the other in many ways, under the sun which gives life to all — held by the earth, that embraces us all.

So how can we engage with our home to nurture our knowing of Home? Simply painting a wall a color with a calming intention creates a more restful bedroom. Paying attention to the arc of the sun and how it activates different rooms throughout the day expands our awareness and unites us with our physical source. Rearranging furniture in our living room allows energy to flow more freely, opening up our life-force. Creating a pond with a small waterfall can bring back soothing memories of childhood, or that same pond and waterfall in an urban backyard can calm the frantic city energy. This work doesn't require more space — it asks us to open our heart to the space within ourselves and our home. There are endless ways to create place, and we can imbue our material world with spirit through our intention and engagement. What we then create can nurture us more fully. Book 2 explores many of these ways.

147

Living into life's paradox, seeking truth rather than convenient answers, presents troubling questions. How do we reconcile living in our lovely homes when the majority of people on the planet barely have a roof over their heads? How do we enjoy the majesty of a forest and then build our home out of wood harvested in a way that decimates those forests? How do we turn on our AC when we know our comfort is made possible because the power plant burns coal that is mined by a process that often blows the tops off of some of the oldest mountains on the planet, that is dangerous to the miners and that pollutes particulates, sickening people with respiratory conditions? You may wonder: How do we even get up in the morning and do anything, knowing we have to consume to live and that our ways of acquiring the resources that feeds us and our houses comes from mostly corrupt sources?

It certainly doesn't help anyone to live in despair, as hard as that may be to avoid. In our heart's stillness — and with time, imagination and the will to grow — we can further awaken to life's harsh realities and, at the same time, the limitless possibilities of reconciliation. We can take each step with the intention of giving of our self to our world as a tree in the forest decomposes to give life to following generations.

We can begin this process — which can heal our self and the world around us — by creating a balanced home, a home with intimacy that is woven into our ecosystem, a home with purpose that helps us find the clarity to step forth and do our life's work.

A STORY AND A PICTURE

There are many ways our buildings can be interwoven into the natural world. The first and essential step is to awaken to this possibility. A simple exploration of this opening: go into the woods, find a small, intimate space, and sit. Be still, and listen. Soften your gaze, or close your eyes. As when dropping a pebble into a still pond, soon your mind will be clear of disturbances. You'll be deep in the pond — the place — and the world around you will begin to embrace you. Animals will resume their goings-on, birds will land on branches nearby; you'll slowly become a part of the place. Then you can begin to consider how the spaces you create and live in can be an extension of this centered place.

In 2010, my wife Beth and I rafted through the Grand Canyon for 18 days. We were outdoors 24 hours a day, in and out of the water, in the canyons formed over billions of years, sleeping under the stars. When we left we were bused to the back of a hotel and told to walk through a hallway up to the lobby to meet another bus. As soon as I entered the hallway, I was completely disoriented, bouncing off walls, head dizzy.

While in the canyons, I had drifted back into some ancient rhythm, or way of being in the world. Every fiber within me was alive, alert, invigorated, breathing, and attuned to the sky and water and canyons. Returning to Cartesian space — abstract and geometric — jarred me out of my found primal existence. I then knew my work was to create spaces where we can be attuned to the sensual, natural world; that the spaces we live in can nourish us, feed our deeper humanity.

As we painfully know, buildings can be life-less and soul-deadening. There is no resonance with anything from the natural world in which we are a part. More acutely, many buildings are full of toxic materials, often hermetically sealed with no relationship to the natural world. Many buildings are designed as discrete objects, with no regard for how the sun tracks across the sky, the wind courses through the windows, the flow of the land, the rhythms of the seasons. Some of us have no awareness of where the building materials come from, or where the energy to feed our buildings come from, or how to block out the summer sun while letting in the winter sun, or how to cool a building by working with the wind.

Again, our home can be a vessel that puts us in more intimate relationship with the world around us, and inspires us to engage with natural energies, flows and rhythms.

We can consider each natural element — water, soil, fire, air/wind, sun, wood, stone — and ask how we can consciously interact with each as we create and live in our homes. Begin this process by thinking of building materials as the food we eat: the more our food lived a healthy life — with no pesticides, hormones, etc.; wasn't processed with chemicals or un-organic additives, etc.; was grown under the sky and fed nurturing food — the more it feeds and nurtures us. Being surrounded by real materials, simply rendered, surrounds us with a vibration or resonance our bodies and minds have always known.

Building forms can be sensual and alive, as our body, not rigid and hard and lifeless. Surfaces can have vitality, hold an intention attuned to what we want to experience in each room: Be soft, or vibrant, or rough, or glassy/reflective/luminous, etc.

In the way that our breath is perhaps our most vital aspect of living, our homes can breathe, drawing in the world around us. Our home can pull in the breezes, and gather daylight deep within. One room can open into a garden, while another expands out to a distant view. Just as we breathe in and out, one space can be expansive, while another space can be inward-focused. Buildings can provide place for inner, reflective solitude, and outward-reaching gatherings.

Our buildings can be as a wave, which is the meeting of the deep energy of the ocean with the firm soil of the earth. A wave puts us in one of the most ancient dynamics of our existence. Our homes can also put us into in-between realms — it can be just inside the edge of a forest overlooking a meadow, or a bay window in a bedroom looking onto a city street — opening up reflective chords, opening us to live deeply.

LIVING AND BUILDING WITH AN
ECOLOGICAL CONSCIOUSNESS

At a green building conference recently, the moderator of a breakout session asked what steps we can take to "build greener." Someone responded, "install solar panels." Someone else suggested we "super-insulate." Another replied, "build with local materials." Appreciating those comments as important considerations, and with some trepidation, I raised my hand and said, "don't build."

(Green, sustainable, ecological, regenerative, etc. — these terms all have different meanings. Trying to clarify each is beyond the scope of this writing. I use "ecologically conscious" as it absorbs all related terms, including Spirit.)

Granted, it seems odd for an architect who makes his living from building to recommend not building. But I went on to say that perhaps 80 percent of the projects our collaborative have worked on over the last 27 years didn't "need" to happen. I told the gathering that when I meet with clients who want to build an addition on their home, I often end up talking them out of building an addition.

Instead, I encourage them to reconsider how they live in the spaces they already have.

The first act of building our home is to develop an ecological consciousness. To consider how we can most innately live, think back to the way we lived as young children — everything appeared to be alive, asking to be engaged with, whether it had a heart or was found under a rock. Children naturally value all things and seek to be a part of their wondrous, mysterious ways of being. This is living as an integral part of our ecosystem.

We can also recognize life is paradox and that there are always issues from both sides — the yin and yang of life — that need consideration. Balance is essential, and we all have to make choices.

We cannot build one hundred percent ecologically for a variety of reasons. It takes great diligence and careful analysis to meet all criteria with every one of the hundreds of choices involved in building. There are many nuances that need to be considered, and some technologies haven't caught up. That said, there are a few essential considerations: responsible use of the earth's resources, or material sourcing; using as little energy as possible, and generating your own energy; and building a healthy, non-toxic home that respects all hands involved in the building, including those at far-away factories and fields. These criteria are augmented by the mantra of "build simply, build small, and build locally."

The creative process of making an ecologically responsive home also explores these considerations —

- If you must build, do not build on untouched land. Consider renovations first, additions second, and then infill lots. Much of our landscape — terrain with human interventions — is a mess, waiting to be redeemed, given new life.

- Live near public transportation — the greenest home in the country uses more energy than a conventional home better connected to public transportation, and close to all types of resources.

- Build your home as part of an ecosystem, not as a discrete object.

- Develop gardens with native plants, implement storm water management stratagies as beautiful landscaping. Collect and use rain water.

- And this is essential — build well, so your home endures for centuries.

- Each of these considerations needs to be balanced with an open-ended design, to fluidly respond to inevitable change.

- Many existing homes simply need to be cracked open, to breathe internally and with the land.

- Small adjustments can go a long way — rather than adding a new space, why not try a bay window in an existing room; or put a new window in a room to expand your home's flow; or repaint an existing space. Or remove a wall or two.

- Or do with less — live more simply and humbly. To be rich is to not want.

To expand these ways, please consider how solar panels spread themselves out, along the earth, to receive the sun. They gather and give free energy, with no emissions, no corrupt systems built around delivering that energy.

We too can expand our heart along the earth, to all, to receive spiritual Light, which we give to our companions. It is pure love-energy, and it's free — we only have to engage and give.

When you begin creating your home, first explore poetic impulses to enliven your home, and try to maintain balance between the pragmatic and the poetic, as two wings of a bird. Consider what Home means as an internal image, and what the land — and existing house, when applicable — is calling for. Perhaps it's the ocean or water that gives you a deep sense of refuge, or maybe it's the stillness of the early morning. Maybe it's an open sky, or a gentle breeze. These life-giving forces can be embodied as the soul of your home. And each place on earth has an equally full personality that offers qualities to be integrated into a home. At its essence, our home can form a union between us and the place in which we dwell. Life is an interconnected web of relationships, and the spaces of our home provide places for our chosen relationships to deepen.

While building is a significant contributing factor of environmental destruction, we need to stop consuming in more significant ways, which go far beyond how we build. So please, before you consider building, ask yourself: first, must you build at all — and if so, what do I really need. Ask as well, how can the home I want help me form deeper relationships with my loved ones, and all occupants of the land in which I dwell. If we try to answer these questions with reverence for the world around us, then through our making and living in our home, we can be more fully alive and become an interconnected part of the web of life.

We can only do what is possible, and feasible, given the spectrum of our whole life. Yet, if we have an ecological awareness and a deep desire to honor all things, we will expand ecological consciousness. Consciousness precedes being — our first, essential work is always to expand consciousness. That deep river will slowly permeate our world, springing up in the making of all homes, and in all of our hearts

BOOK IV

LEARNING TO LOVE A FOREST

Prologue

In God's wildness lies the hope of the world — the great fresh unblighted, unredeemed wilderness. The galling harness of civilization drops off, and wounds heal ere we are aware.
— John Muir, co-founder of the Sierra Club, mystic

The forest we live in is no longer wildness. My wife, Beth, and I are loving the forest, letting the forest return to its essence after being blighted by human hands. Perhaps the forest is a young wildness. I know the forest's and our consciousness is wildness. The healing Muir is calling for is our estrangement from the earth.

There's a light grain seed inside, You fill it with yourself, or it dies.
I'm caught in this curling energy! Your hair!
Whoever's calm and sensible is insane!
— Rumi, Sufi mystic

I am so small, I can barely be seen. How can this great Love be inside me?
— Rumi

160

Muir understood the earth is a living, spiritual being. Through my time in a forest, I've experienced that I share the same source, Spirit, that can be accessed through *our light grain seed.* I can engage with the forest, form relationship, *fill it with yourself* and further know *this great Love.* Love is truth, known through relationship. I am learning to love a forest.

Teilhard de Chardin, the French Jesuit priest and theologian, offered *You are not a human being in search of a spiritual experience. You are a spiritual being immersed in a human experience.* I can live through Spirit in many ways. My intention with this book is to offer ways with a forest. Humans have been a part of nature for 10,000 generations; it's only been the last few generations that we have lost our connection.

I find little more fulfilling than experiencing a forest's deeper presence, as currents in the ocean. Through stillness, opening my heart and listening, I can connect, Dwell with these life-forces. I offer two ways to form relationship — sit in a small place, a vestibule, a portal into the forest; or go on silent, centered, open-ended ambles. For both ways we can receive and record voices (take notes), then go home, sit down, light a candle — a door into Spirit — and begin writing. Or paint, or dance, or...

Our world is waking up to seeking reciprocity in all walks and ways of life. I can be part of a mutual relationship with nature, equally giving to each other. I can protect the forest, as the forest welcomes me. I can give voice to the forest. I can ask the forest what it wants, beyond to be with me.

Learning to Love a Forest is an account of a love affair. Beth and I moved here in 2019; she is the fourth generation in her family to live here. For the first fifteen years of our marriage I didn't even want to come here. Being a Californian, nothing about all of this endless rolling greenness spoke to me. Then in the next five years a slow opening rose in my heart. I dare say the forest called me here, and I said, "yes!"

For nearly two years I ventured into our forest every day, rain or shine, freezing or hot. I ambled, sat, danced, smiled, grateful for efts and fungi and trees and flowers and boulders and brooks. I followed the call of hermit thrushes, was astonished by tree trunk

161

sculpture, roots enveloping boulders, leaves gathering sunlight. I played in three feet of snow and splashed through saturated life.

Memories of my beloved, raw, varied, powerful American Southwest, where I learned to walk and years later respond to Spirit awakening me, began fading. I was in the forest, the forest was in me — I began falling in love with this forest. I always trust when life takes me where I never thought I'd go.

Forest in Prose

The forest we dwell in is a landscape, touched by many hands.

Vermont has been populated for nearly 13,000 years. The remaining tribe, the Abenaki Nation, went the way of most native people when European settlers arrived. Vermont was then mostly forested, although subtly manipulated by the Abenaki. Settlers quickly cut down many trees for fuel, building, and to make room for farming. Subsequent immigrants continued treating the forests as a commodity. Through it all, considerable forests have returned.

The forest has memories of logging roads, vague tire ruts as vegetation and erosion have given them no preferential treatment. Most noticeable are stone walls, all originally about three feet tall. These too are slowly dissolving into the earth, and the earth and her fingers — mostly moss and lichen — are swarming over the stone walls. Peace is returning.

As I amble through the forest, the roads and walls startle me as they speak of purpose, rationality, destruction. Yet in a sense, they were planted and are engaging with the forest, not so differently from a fallen tree (lichen slowly breaks down stone). And the walls can be comforting when I'm feeling lost or tired.

The forest is full of such dualities, showing me that life is a complex equation. Boulders are swallowed by the earth; trees' octopus-roots crawl around boulders; rocky brooks carved by water; trees standing when they're dead, still giving life to many beings; beavers killing trees to create ponds, become courtyards for numerous creatures to find sustenance; cold, hard boulders give softness and gentleness to the forest.

Some parts of the forest are open, some closed. Some dark, some light. Some wet, some dry. Some flat, some rolling. Some sweet, some pungent. Some mysterious, some neutral. Some earthy, some airy. Some challenging, some comforting. All essential.

Spring teases, gives bit by bit of renewal as it pleases. Don't hold your breath. And watch that mud, and those black flies!

In summer green is growing on green on green, held by a blue sky. Its beauty balances its brevity. Don't mind those pesky deer flies!

Fall begins in August. Fall is death falling on death, flaming out. Warns us of winter.

In winter everything is exposed and shivering. And thickly white, trying to survive. Yet transcendent.

The other ancient beings on this land keep themselves hidden. Other than eagles, hawks, owls, crows, turkeys, grouse, and migratory birds, we rarely see any animals. Visible are their tracks in the snow or mud. An unofficial survey — moose, bears, deer, raccoons, rabbits, coyotes, mice, weasels, beavers, chipmunks, red squirrels.

I love the disorder of the forest, and its complexities. Everything is growing everywhere

all wanting to live.

DWELLING
Filling It With Ourself

While in the forest, I'm learning that I am nature — there is no separation. I'm beckoned to be my true self. I can be in intimate relationship with the forest. The forest is a door into my Home, my still, silent center, where my light grain seed resides.

Please consider that "life" is the fullness and union we seek with truth, known through love. The world we believe is the life we live. The world is constantly trying to distract us from truth, luring us with false light, material temptations. Dwelling centers our living, keeps us aligned in Spirit's light, in-lightens us, clarifies our light grain seed through which we radiate light and love to the earth and our companions.

I'm learning I can vitalize and expand my life by engaging and forming relationship with a forest. I seek to live as a child, activating and finding life within any aspect of the forest, and discover wonder in every particle.

The world is alive beyond what we can see. An artist opens their mind and heart and body, brings love and light into the world. We are all artists! Art reveals truth, isn't interested in being pretty.

Our light grain seed illumines every moment. My heart is opening to expert-Ence the life within the forest.

A Few Windows Into Dwelling
Impulses Within Ways to Form Relationship With a Forest

I offer images, seeds that we can internalize and sprout into ways to Dwell in a forest. A candle — a single lit candle gathers presence. It centers us, creates an opening for Spirit to enter. Our light grain seed is a candle flame. Spirit is the candle.

A flower — a flower lifts its entire self to the sun, arcing with the sun. It absorbs the sun, radiates Spirit's light and vibration. So can we.

A sailboat — we tend to be in the world as when riding in a powerboat. We unconsciously flip on switches, rely on opaque technology with little regard for the world around or in us. We can be enlivened as when sailing, paying attention to the world and responding.

A wave — a wave forms union between the mysterious ocean depths and the shore. Being in this in-between space expands us, where we become the wave.

WAYS

Rumi offers an incantation for forming relationship with a forest — there are hundreds of ways to kneel and kiss the earth. As love is a verb, we can love, engage with, Dwell in a forest. As with human beings, love begins and is centered in opening our heart to the other.

SOME (OF THE HUNDREDS OF) WAYS TO LOVE A FOREST

Settle into a place in the forest. As a drop in a pond, let our entry-ripples flow out as vibrations, uniting us as they penetrate the forest. Open to relationship with all life we meet — sit with them, enter their pulse into mutual inner silence. Listen. As is true for humans, a forest's soul resides in silence. From this still place, love is born.

Set out on an amble, an engaging, discovering, exploring, mindful meditative journey. An amble is not a hike, nor a walk. It is gently kissing the earth with no intention or direction other than to follow invitations to enter relationship with the forest. An amble is making love — feeling an intimate impulse, responding to enter into what that opening offers.

The forest and all of its beings breathes. Air unites us. Focus on our breath, with deep inhales, gathering in; and exhales, releasing. Let the rhythm arise that comes from the forest.

Respond to and expand the life-force we hear calling in a place in the forest. Build a fairy home, or make nature art (as Andy Goldsworthy) — a cairn that evolves into sculpture, or a sculpture from fallen branches, or…

Put feet in a brook, or pond. Let the water get to know us, energetically flow through us. Our feet turn liquid. Slowly our deeper currents align. If the water is deep enough, enter with our whole body.

Listen for the bird songs, they bring Spirit's voice. Sing or whistle with them! Learn their calls, what they're saying.

Sing hymns to the forest. The forest absorbs holy vibrations, will join in via the wind in the trees or water running through a brook, or...

Write and sing chants in places in the forest we hear calling for healing. They can be as brief as a single work, such as ""home," or "love." Chants gather life-force, fill a space with spiritual energy.

Open vision to gazing, a soft, receptive way to look into the forest depths. Where life flows in and through all beings. Feel ourself dissolve into the swirl. See as Van Gogh.

Let our body respond to the forest. Stand, close eyes, and begin any movement we feel the forest and our body asking for. Once we begin, our body takes us where the forest offers. Dance, sing, drum...

Sleep in the forest, be together in our dreams. Our body absorbs nature's rhythms and forces, awake or asleep.

The following poems offer fruit from these ways. They form an ecosystem; all equal, none separate.

When forming a relationship with a forest, sometimes I don't feel or see or hear anything. That's okay. I know as I engage with the forest, I am forming relationship. I know that sitting or walking and feeling the beauty in a forest brings solace and some healing, deepens and expands my and a forest's life.

Bird's call say, "rejoice!" Wind in trees say, "isn't this exhilarating, living life!" Water flowing over rocks in brook say, "listen to my music!" A forest implores us to engage and live, invites us to enter and be a part of its hidden wonders, flashes of truth.

POEMS

PRELUDE

171

An Amble Through the Forest – First Date

August 30th, 2019

My first encounter with the forest was ecstatic — a universe opened up, my heart expanded — setting the tone for our unfolding relationship.

A vibration swells within

when truth rises. Ambling,
knowing forest calls.

Life mingling with death.

Yielding trees with life growing in, on —
softly glowing fungi, many mosses,
infant trees with two perfect leaves,
back to back, taking in all

they face to find sky.

Small cracks come to life.

Voice after voice calls.
Slow step by slow step
on leaf-layered, warming
earth's membrane. Pulled
to a boulder engulfed in green.

Globe of life

entangled in tree's octopus roots.

Ferns, gentle breaking waves.
Hemlocks gather, lure with scented needle beds.

I'm a lightening rod, receiving life.

Starlit sky of life forms
communicating, collaborating.

A cappella hymn.

Strong winds sweep overhead, gather
branches in sashaying swarms.

Light riding wind.

Barely standing trees gesture anguish
as struck warriors, brave guardians

uniting sun and earth.

THRESHOLD

Expanding Love

September 2nd, 2019

Forest weaves many brooks
gently calling. Sleeping baby,
        all calms.

        Brooks explore,
reveal rocks and stories —
singing water pulled
over rock ledge after ledge after ledge.

Trees rise to sun. Light penetrates
tree's fullness — life-beams absorbed
in layers of leaves.

Rounding boulders from earth's womb
        shaped by time.

Earth's green blanketing
        purls wind and sunlight.

Splash of light finds me.

Cloud of tiny white fairy-moths swirl
        in light. Become light.

Wind picks up, life flows into life.
Van Gogh.

I join,
standing, rooting, swirling
arms as branches, hands as leaves.

Always changing
light, clouds, wind, leaves, brook's mood.
I'm given a moment,
a ring in tree's life.

Joy

July 1st, 2020

Ahhh   gentle breeze greets leaves
and me

Forest kiss!

There are endless ways we can kiss the earth, and the forest has its ways to kiss us —

The sparkling sun through tree boughs; a cool, big-bellied boulder to rest on in summer; a misty waterfall to refresh us; a cool pond to dive into as we greet the day, fully awakening us…

This can go on all day! Can you tell me a few ways you especially love a forest, and have been loved by a forest?

And where does the breeze's life-force come from? Sure science has an answer, but when we're in the experience, we can open our heart into the spiritual aspect. We can feel the forest's warm lips on our forehead, blessing us.

Look Into My Light

July 3rd, 2020

Forest's voice reflecting within sun
playing on brook's waters speckled glass.
Blinding light burned into me

Look into My light.

Gazing in —
        absolution.

        Seeking solace
from dark forces, unavoidable currents.

You're a light-bulb fish in ocean depths —
        Shine!

Peace

July 19th, 2020

Ambling to Threshold, calling
       hermit thrush.
She delivers preamble.

Brook offers fluid incense.
Cherry fungi, living candles.

Slight breeze in branches.
Forest dreams.

Submerged feet. Soon
they're water, clear.

Silence lifts veil into peace.
Filled
       sap in tree.

Prodigal Son
August 8th, 2020

Enduring a storm within, and out.

Summer-filled butterfly bids

    Return to forest.

Ecstatic butterfly prophets visited earlier —
       sun orgy, burst of joy.

Sky cleared, as did path.

Arriving, little breeze.
Trees greet
       with shy waves.

Feet in brook, splashing peace.

Silence opened.

Something released. Cleared,
       returned Home.

AMBLES

When It's Time
July 2nd , 2020

Drop
        of water, held
in leaf after storm, going
where wind blows
when it's time

        to leave. Seeking

Home,
absorbed in earth.

This poem was written by a drop of water. As I gazed into it, this poem poured out.

Dwelling opens our path to Home. Our material Home is the earth; it's where our bodies came from and will return to. But the earth is also a portal to our spiritual Home, when we're absorbed in the earth at death. And we can access Home anytime through the earth.

We are held in the earth — she is our refuge. Yet strong winds blow, which we need to return Home. Otherwise, we stay nestled in and evaporate, rotting our home. Life is as ephemeral as a drop of water, and equally life-giving.

By leaving, we can arrive, and when the wind blows is as mysterious as Home.

I Know My Place
July 10th, 2020

Ambling
low branch appears.

Bow.   Over and over.

The Latin root for humility is "ground," which can be extrapolated to "earth." When I'm in the forest, I'm opening to being an integral part of the forest — to be as all aspects of the forest, respecting and honoring each other. Take away any of the multitude of forest beings, and it's incomplete. I'm a part, no more important than any other.

Amidst the cultural debate re: appropriate pronouns, I advocate "we." We are all we; there is no I.

185

A Glimpse of Eternity
July 19th, 2020

Ambling, every step has never been taken.

No one has been here. And here…

No one has heard wind play with trees
this way. No one
has seen this light on leaves.

Forest doesn't know time.

Hymn of Devotion

July 24th, 2020

On thin stalk, almost not there
small tall flower strives, seeks sun.
Amid powerful winds
devotion stays true.

Protected by love-force.

Trees, older, wiser
with leaves as petals
opening to light.

Flowers prance their devotion, trees drum.

Boulders gave their liquid-life,
hold all still.
Slowly covered, soon
forgotten.

Brook's water gives
itself, pulled
to ocean.

Renewed, spawns life.

Gratitude

July 25th, 2020

The earth is 4.54 billion years old.

Green Mountains, once
taller than Rockies, since calmed
      by two Ice Ages. Now
gentle rolling old beings.

Forest, comforting coverlet.

Soil, earth's skin, thickening
since Her first breaths.
          Creation's dust.

      Water
older than earth — arrived
on asteroid — tirelessly
assumes any shape asked.

Boulders burst out near the beginning,
        twice enduring
glacier's grinding, wind and water's rubbing.

Becoming sand, particles of praise.

Trees, recent, sprout quickly, feed earth.
Each leaf adoring sun.

Ferns pulsate with wind.
Dinosaurs trampled, I tip-toe
lessening impact.

I am so small, how is it I'm here?

You're My moon, reflecting
My light.

Balance
August 7th, 2020

Brook's stone edge holds
        young tree.

Precarious, given brook's many minds.

Ten feet up, splits in two.
One up, one arcs across brook.

One emphatic, one elegant.
One firm, resolute, one creating as it goes.
Yang, Yin.

Fred and Ginger.

Each Drop More

October 22nd,2020

Raindrop, clinging
to bare limb
            holds its world.

            Each tree a universe.

Forest floor shimmers —
slippery, slidey, spongy.

Soil's essence, scent
seeps to surface.

Deep inhale, expanding in.

Close, soft, thick clouds
with multitude of blessings.
            Raining.

Forests Don't Grieve

October 28th, 2020

Life doesn't end, nor does death.

>   Everything
living, dying. New life, dead life
side by side, not afraid of other.

Shredding tree shows
life's spiral. Decomposing
with more to say —
>   Pieta
raw, challenging, revealing beauty amid suffering.

Standing perishing trees give life. Opened,
feeding bacteria, fungi, insects, woodpeckers.
Trunks, modern sculpture —
>   Giacometti!

Loggers leave tree stumps for dead
>   becoming
templums for many tiny green beings
creating other worlds.

Islands of wonder.

Small tree, my height, with lifeless arm-branches
arcing upwards — dancer's grace
is still, yet not
          as my joining enlivens.

Tree melts into earth
          becomes
food for its offspring, continues living through them.

Scarred tree's wound opens
into wild expression — vaginal portal
into deeper presence, bellows

          Live! You are alive!

Snowy Woods

January 24th, 2021

Scentless
        clear ice air deep in lungs.

Silence.

Pregnant sky.

Snow on land, engulfing nuance. Diamond sea
with gentle swells, reflects
skies' hidden colors.

Blue streaks reveal white's secrets.

Winter, expansive, exposing
animal's lives, tree's intricacies and expressions.
Low sun's pearly shrouding clouds
        slipping through trees.

Trees float, aloof, hide behind each other.
        Ascending strokes —
burnt umber, charcoal, yellow ochre, aged moss,
        puzzle of greys.

Bark flakes circling trunks. Always feeding others.

Evergreen charades.

Birch leaves, stubborn, refused fall, yield
to winter storms, illuminate layers of snowfall.
            Ethereal fossils.

Brooks close in, earth's sinuous eyes.
            Calligraphy. Impulsive.

            Boulders feign mountains.
Moose drag hoofs.
Deer walk attentively, surely, no distractions.
Turkeys skate.

Red squirrels skittle,
form circuits, link trees.

Coyotes, together, and not.
Their urine, maple yellow, liquid soil.
Their scat, one dark, one light.
No blood. Prey safe.

Gravity concentrates snow's light.
Blustery swirls gather light flakes.

Wind softens presence, tells time.
Snow falls, peace reigns.
            Vision becomes internal.

April, Early May
April 22nd, 2021

Darkness.

Held in mother

aspiring green begins.
Crown appears, baby pulled
by light.

Sun.
Sooner, sooner
arcing to zenith.

Fertile brooks, tender soil protected by tired leaves,
pool after pool reflecting empty trees.

Eager flowers, light's scouts.

Cocooned leaves intricately unfold.
Exhaling, billowing sails.

Unfurling love.

Early August
Early August, 2021

Fall quietly slides under summer.

Summer's abundance insists, wanting
life even when sun says otherwise.

Sun strongly slants into leaves, giving
another radiance.
Yellow thinly inscribes green, seeping.

Prophetic hue-filled leafs land, joining fungi
as earth's rainbow,
beguiling fading leaf veneer.

Ferns current flows, luffing.
Maple saplings, hives of newborns, play in soil
knowing it's soon time to go home.

Rains wane, rivulets become
paths, tell water's story.

Summer's sweet scent begins
wafting leaf's last life-force.

Memories of other seasons kaleidoscope.

CHAPELS

Chapels Build Themselves

October 25th, 2019

After giving every drop of sunlight

leaf can to its tree,
it dangleslets   go   falls.

Each landing is an altar

where leaf returns Home,
          its essence
next blessing as rain or wind or…

Life surrenders ascension, builds chapels.

Tree falls, lays, melts into earth, becomes
island of life feeding Mother.
          Fairies' playground.

Elephantine boulders, mountain hearts.

Ponds gather life.

Hemlock cloisters offer refuge.

Enclosing trees protect
intimate silent meadows,
            halos of light.

Ambling, chapel to chapel —
        beggar seeking alms

Beyond

October 28th, 2019

Ambling, concealed door opens in forest's bedlam.

Come. Enter.

Mossy green everywhere, soft small
luminous dewdrop petals.

Fairies flutter in flashes of light.

Pan hides in trees, his flute rides breeze.

Firm old wise hemlocks guard
small silent reflecting pools.
Fallen trees give refuge.

Spring of wonder, timeless,
       still
with humming whisper —

     Stay

Sacred Grove

October 24th, 2019

The Sacred Grove is a story of redemption.

Beth's grandfather allowed part of his land to be quarried for gravel for an improved state highway just above their property. Half of the hill is gone, a deep scar. But he then planted over a hundred red pine trees, on a grid. This occurred sixty years ago; now, the grove is transcendent.

The Sacred Grove is a cathedral. Such groves inspired Gothic cathedrals.

Forest loves Grove, offers pilgrimage.

Crossing rocky brooks awakens.
Rustle of leaves cleanses.
Climbing hills enlivens.
Milkweed seed-puffs float, embodied fairies,
heart opens.

Uplifting silence embraces arrival.

      Gentle silence, soft exhale.

      Loving silence, warmth.

Ambling on cloud
        of needles. Trunks swim,
swirling currents.

Slanting sun's duet,
        light and shadow playing trunks.

Trunks rise sixty focused feet, chanting

        Rise! Gather sun!

Columns root in lightly rolling land,
childish grid.

Everything vibrates.

Trees, wind's barometer, timidly sway
with each other. Shy orgy.
        Wind, a hymn.

Nothing dare interrupt.

Leave?
July 2nd, 2020

Song from forest's depths

plaintive, haunting, entrancing, primal,
          longing beyond forest.

Hermit thrush calls.

Turning, there's a baby brook
with just enough water to live.

        Gentle voice.

        Delicate softness.

Leave?

Mind responds
There are things to do, return.

Heart says
Go ahead, now you know what you'll miss.

Over and over, mind clutters.
Heart becomes.

Finally, mind insists it's time to go home.
Heart says

   You are.

GROUND

Amidst
July 10th, 2020

A nested spider's perfection

       Still.

       Silent.

       Centered.

       Attentive.

       Patient.

       Meticulous.

       Articulate.

       Resilient.

within wind, world in turmoil.

Dreams
July 11th, 2020

   Trees serve forest as
laying down to sleep.

   Out of their dreams rise fungi.

Shy, enchanting
flowers breathing.

Their name gives joy.

Fungi doesn't care. It just glows
   colors unseen elsewhere.

Last light trees have to offer.

Love

July 12th, 2020

Where does flower end sun begin?

In our heart.

I love the simplicity and power of this poem. I can still see the flower that whispered these words to me. I only heard them as my heart was open. The sun warmed us, and the earth held us.

An open flower mirrors the sun's orb. As with the moon, I take in the sun's light reflecting off the flower into my heart. There it is planted, to grow as Spirit's light and love to radiate from my heart and smile.

Solace
July 12th, 2020

Floating through
sea of ferns

      caressing angel wings.

When in need of solace, I often find myself floating, not grounded, drifting mindlessly, wanting a divine touch. The forest holds many experiences and moods, and a meadow of ferns, especially on a breezy day, is full of angels gentling fanning their love to all in need.

Whenever you're in need of solace and can't access a meadow of ferns, enter through meditation — picture the meadow, see the sea of ferns transform into angel wings, feel the angel's love. Rest in this knowing.

Safety

July 12th, 2020

Inchworm visits, drops in
         out of sky.

         With no eyes
he senses his way. He does his
up and down walk, up and down, pausing
when he feels me.

Feeling safe he continues.

That moment of safety was love.

Helping him stretch onto a leaf, he blindly wanders
reaching for foothold, leaving
security in each step.

Courage?

He's just doing what he's here to do.
         This he sees clearly.

Another inchworm visits. I brusquely
move him aside. Forest feels my remorse,
         sends forgiving breeze.

Love In Every Step

July 13th, 2020

Efts, juvenile newts, seemingly bred
with fungi, their luminosity
            as mysterious. Precious

as ruby, new born, snow flake.
Found on forest floor, vibrant
as fallen fall leaf.

They ask for love in our every step.

Freedom

July 19th, 2020

Fallen tree cedes into earth.

When does it stop being
        tree, becomes soil?

We die, bodies become soil, freeing
us to find Home.

We never stop being.

How to Live

August 1st, 2020

Butterflies, folding paper,
       fly pluckily, pierce strong winds,
skip along garden flowers
       unconcerned.

Monarchs, from Mexico!

I Will Happen
August 18, 2020

I'm tired

of waiting
for my time, freedom
to fly to my destiny.

To float aimlessly to a small place.

I dream of my moment
daily, nightly, as I watch other seeds
loft away.

Dreams bring solace, but no deliverance.

I will find Home
where potent nucleus of life

I am

can happen. Can become
after burrowing into earth, finding
foothold, twisting into position,

reaching out of the womb.

Fall's First Gestures

August 29th, 2020

Leaf's spine sunrays reaching tree's roots.

Late summer, leaf falls,
its reds and oranges and yellows
melting away summer's green
        from inside.

Spring's innocent light green
darkens to summer's demands,
pales at summer's end,
        becomes earth.

Some green leaves dropped away
not wanting to endure fire.

Ferns boisterous splaying begins
loosing buoyancy, seas calming.

Summer slowly surrenders to earth's reversal.
Waning sunlight secretes sap into earth.

Growing life sighs. Relieved,
their devotion to sun goes inside.
        Rest. Fortify.

Center Holds Peace

December 18th, 2020
For Matthew

Forest has endless trees,
each unique, precious.

The more unique, the more precious.

Wind's roaring currents sway tree tops.
Then calm. Then wind. Then calm…

Center holds peace.

Boulder dissolves into its source
            patiently, silently
through rain and moss.
            Pain and loss.

No weight remains when we give ourself.

We awake in our Home

where peace resides.

Wind can't blow this away.

One Light

January 16th, 2021

Snow falls.
Snow melts.

I'll die.

Falling snowflake, cryptic crystal,
Love's light.

No other as me. Ever.

Seeking firm ground to rest.
Return Home.

Snow Leaving
March 27th, 2012

        Illuminating,
softening, slowing, transforming, shrouding.

Lover pulls back cover, awakening
        her beloved.

Earth's rotation returns sun, lazily
returns earth. White dreams
give way to swarms of textures, multitudes
        of renewal.

Soft breeze, gaining light, warmth.

Scents returning, earth exhaling.
Birds returning, enlivening air.

White opens to patches of earth, soon
to be islands.
        Soon gone.

        Weary grey
trees long for leaves' return.

Fallen leaf carpet swims
into liquid sheets, gathering into brooks.
Brooks learn river's ways.
        Whisper to roar. Gentle to emphatic.

Burrowed green remembers sun, gathers
last essence before another cycle.

Snow flakes give way to snow drops.
Flattened ferns wait for sun resurrecting.
Growing snow rings at tree base
        melted by returning sap.
Trees that were buried bow.

Last taste of winter, melting crystals
        illuminating.

First Breath

April 9th, 2021

Soul in darkness.
Unknowing. Enduring. Within
            vast void.

            Not boundless,
held in ocean.

Tide does change, unseen
celestial forces.

Moon holds rhythms.
Constellations comfort.
Planets, true companions.
Comets seek refuge.

Home slowly warms.
First breath, wanting.

Returning green fills earth,
bird songs fill air,
frogs fill water,
flowers fill heart.

Light fills soul.

ADDENDUM

DEVELOPING AWARENESS
Opening Ourself to Dwell Everyday, Everywhere

OPEN UP TO AND BREATHE IN THE BEAUTY AND POWER OF NATURE

Attentive actions, deeply entering the one thing we're doing, reveals truth. Such as eating in silence, honoring all that went into our meal arriving in our bowl; or cooking with gratitude for all aspects of our sustenance, prepared lovingly.

Spirit is in the shine of the sun, moon, stars, and is in the wind.

We can —

- Feel, breathe in, be invigorated by, the life-force within the wind.
- Observe the many ways life reaches up to our source, the sun.
- Observe the play of light on form, how the sun knows itself. Light gives life. Nature absorbs, transforms, praises the sun.
- Consider the moon, the mystery of its light, power over the earth, its relationship with the earth and sun. Open and receive the astonishing light, from the sun, reflecting off the moon.
- Observe forces imbued in a forest, such as decomposition, growth, gravity, weather, wind, cold and heat, rain…
- Play with nature. Splash in water, body surf, hike in rugged places (fear awakens us),- jump into a pile of leaves, roll in the mud, dig into the earth and feel the soil and the millions of organisms …

224

Attune With Nature's Rhythms

We can consider how every day is a microcosm of our life. As is true for nature, our life unfolds cyclically. Through each incarnation, we rise from darkness (wake up), live and grow under the sun (play out each day), and return to the earth (go to bed).

Life has ebbs and flows, waves (intense time of activity) are followed by a pause, four sea- sons… Rather than willing our way through, we can embrace and allow ourself to live into these rhythms. We can —

- Greet morning, midday, evening. Observe how each calls different aspects of ourself. Feel the rhythm of hope at sunrise, and the uncertainty of darkness at sunset.
- Enter into each season, observe changes, large and small, within ourself, our home and in our place. We burst open in summer, go inward in winter, reflect on our loses in fall, are reborn in spring.
- Enjoy the sensuality of each season. Be with a fire in winter, float in water in summer….
- Flow with the weather, let ourself feel heavy on cloudy days, and rejoice as a bird song when sunny. We are the weather, nature, the earth. We feel their forces as they are in us. We're all stardust.
- Know our water's journey, how it comes to us, nurtures us, returns to the ocean.
- Track the moon's monthly journey, know where it rises and sets, if its arc is high or low, how it's luminous shape changes.
- Observe migrating birds, their arrival, their actions, their songs; their departure.
- Plant and tend a garden — most cogently teaches nature's rhythms and ways.

A Few Ways to Dwell in Our Daily Walk

Given our forgetfulness, here are a few ways to help us remember to walk through the world   with a poet's eyes, a child's sense of wonder. We can —

- Begin by greeting the morning, give gratitude for the gift of life. Then through yoga, meditation, etc., we can align ourself with Spirit. Once centered, we can walk listening for Spirit to offer insights; and respond.
- Listen for the bird songs, they call for the sun to rise, and the new day. They're messengers, coming to us throughout the day, calling us Home.
- Observe the ways light meets the earth. We see through light coming into our eyes; what we see also enters our being. Water's expressions embody light's quality, leaves are slivers of light, city streets are kaleidoscopes of light.
- Deeply take in those flowers we walk by, give them a greeting. Their purpose is to open to, and give color to light. So is ours.
- Try not to walk with our head down, lost in our thoughts. Try to look up and see what is really there, the beauty within.
- Consider that no matter how denuded a landscape is, the clouds are Spirit's luminosity, a constant reminder of Spirit all around us.
- Know that fierce wind is Spirit's cleansing breath, invigorating us.
- Carry a song or hymn with us, swimming in its love.
- Listen for a playground if feeling lost. Let the children's joy seep into us…go swing!
- Daydream, let our mind wander as a raft in the ocean, perhaps laying down on soft grass looking up into the clouds. Our mantra is often, "life is full." It can be, "life is precious, every moment." Give the weight we feel to the earth; she welcomes us. Draw up her loving embrace.
  - Smile! Smiling melts away any un-ease, returns us to who we are — a radiant being bringing love and light to our companions and earth.

A FEW LAST WORDS

END NOTES, ABOUT BEGINNINGS

Filling our light grain seed, and building the world in Love through Dwelling, can be part of our life. Yet living in Love is work — we want a happy and peaceful life, but that pearl lives amidst an often turbulent ocean, within our self, and in the world. Our deeper Self wants to live a real, fully human life, embracing everything we encounter. There are no extraneous encounters we're offered, nor are there coincidences.

The other work we do, our occupation, is just a wire, a medium to carry a current — Love — from our Source to our companions. Our jobs are important — regardless of societal values, they are all equal, essential strands in our material ecosystem

— but our real work is to give love to each other, always, and support each other as we suffer doing the deeper work we incarnated to do. We're all healing, seeking to reconnect with who we truly are.

To end, a few words on beginning your day. These following practices can align us with our Source, and help us swim in its ocean all day. But we're human with destiny, karma and wounds, which attempt to act through us. These practices help center us, giving us solid ground to walk through our day, facing all of its challenges.

Each dawn is the dawning of creation — we are reborn each morning. Dawn is our moment to again experience our central existential reality — our life is infinite and eternal, and we are very small. What primarily keeps us from living into limitless possibilities — where we expand as part of it all — are our false mental constructs and our stale stories.

The breeze at dawn has secrets to tell us — try to get up at the crack of dawn, each day's portal. Go to a small space oriented to the rising sun — give gratitude for its return, and for having made it through the night. Be still, try to quiet your mind. Enter silence, within which resides your Self. Open your heart. Pay attention to the earth's awakening — the birds calling, the quality of light, your neighbor going out to get his newspaper — and yours.

Breathe. Breathe in and out — take in the fresh morning, exhale that which no longer serves you — with the pulse of the earth.

Connect with peace's vibration with a simple chant, such as "om." Feel this vibration reverberate throughout your body and fill your home. If the time calls for it during the day, reside in peace by closing your eyes, taking a deep breath, and exhale from a guttural place, where peace's vibration lays waiting.

Just as the heat of the rising sun makes thermals that flow into wind, begin moving your body with the flow of the earth. Become the wind. Expand your movement to a body/mind/spirit practice, such as yoga or Tai Chi. Activate and open all parts of yourself, clarifying your heart and body for more light to radiate.

Call in your spiritual guardians and guides. You have them, even if you don't know them. Have gratitude for their being with you. Make a vow for how you want to live in the world. Ask for your awareness to be elevated, to Spirit, so you may know the brilliance of the beauty you love. Ask your questions and go out and live into them. Ask your guardians and guides for their support throughout the day.

From this centered place, walk through the world with your poet's eyes, your child's sense of wonder.

Listen to the birds calling forth the sun and the new day. Birds are messengers throughout the day, each song calling us Home. Or observe a flower — its primary purpose is to open to, and give color to, light. So is ours.

Walk with your head up, taking in the world, each moment. It's so easy to find our head down, lost in thought, disconnected from the world around us.

No matter how denuded a landscape you find yourself in, the clouds are Spir- it's luminosity — a constant reminder of its presence all around us.

That fierce wind that slows you down or chills you is Spirit's breath cleansing and invigorating you.

Sing — carry a song or hymn with you, swimming in its Love. If you begin

229

to get lost, let a song arise to bring you back to your Self.

When needing to re-center, I simply repeat "calm center," in rhythm with my breathing.

Walk through a park where children play. Let their joy seep into you — and go for a swing!

When feeling stressed, lie on your back, be held by — and give the pressure you're feeling to — the earth. We can free our self. You can also find a tree and spend a few minutes sitting against it. Feel its life force; ask it to fill you. Look up and see the dappled light, a veil to higher realms where your Home resides.

Or just daydream — let your mind float with the clouds. We're so busy; peace is underneath all that activity. Our mantra is often "life is full." We can live by "my life is in every moment." Everything we need to know is in each moment's space, where we are, as the rose, unfurling through Your Love.

It's so easy to be pulled away from our Source — our material realm is constantly trying to distract us, and there is our unruly mind. Firmness is primary, but not rigid — reside in balanced yin and yang. Stay tuned to the music, keep your beat, feel the flow.

Like all practices, these take time to develop — I first awakened to this work in 1989, and I'll be charting my constellation, Dwelling, for the rest of my life.

Every breath throughout our day is in gratitude — "I am so small, I can barely be seen/ How is this great Love in me?"

DWELLING LIVES ON OUR WEBSITE & THROUGH WORKSHOPS

Dwelling is an alive possibility — there are infinite ways to Dwell. A book is, in some ways, static in form. My intention then for the website is to give voice to the open current of Dwelling. Please join me there, in our Dwelling community, where we can share our stories of our home, and journey Home.

Please visit our website — www.exploringdwelling.com where you will find:

Book page - with links to purchase the book and a brief bio about Bill Hutchins.
Community page - with a growing library of inspirational stories about explorations, experiences and spaces, as well as a link to our Facebook community (please like our page on FB and share with others!):
- Interviews with poets, spiritual teachers and home dwellers, amongst others.
- News of interesting projects and provocative work by others.
- Readers' stories of making Home, through their home.
- Beams of Love (blog posts) — brief offerings exploring Dwelling.
Movement page — with news about upcoming workshops and events where we look forward to meeting you!

Please go on the website to continue exploring Dwelling and engage with other Dwellers. We will be presenting themes and asking for your input so we can all expand each other. We look forward to your comments, suggestions or anything else about Dwelling. Write to us you would like to share your story, experience, or video with us.

WORKSHOPS

Ultimately, Dwelling can only be learned through doing. I offer workshops that, in very simple ways, can help you experience Dwelling, that you can then take home to live into.

The workshops begin with reading "A Seed for Dwelling," where a space is opened with a candle. We then do a number of the explorations from Book 2. These creative-expressions are intended to reveal your life-giving impulses, and we then discuss how they can be embodied in your home, and the way you live there.

Duration of the workshop depends on participant's intentions — how deeply you want to go into this work. As with all workshops, the real work is what you do after a workshop. I'm available to participants long after a workshop.

The workshop forms -

I offer a one-day workshop at my home, which embodies Dwelling.

I offer a one-day workshop with you and your family at your home.

I can offer the one-day workshop at your home, where you invite friends to join us. Everyone would get to explore Home for themselves, and we'd focus on ways you can further Dwell in your home.

Expanding that workshop, I offer a series of 4 workshops, for 4 people or couples, rotating from house to house, season after season.

The workshop can begin with a Friday night talk, followed by a day-long workshop, or a couple of days, or a week.

I team with a healer or teacher doing parallel work. With you?

I offer the workshop to architects, to give them other ways to know their clients.

Please contact me at Bill@exploringdwelling.com if interested. I'm happy to travel to offer Dwelling, as well as give tours of my home and get to know you!

GRATITUDE

I am a few communities

That have blown wind into my journey Home,
Centered around my family.
Within my family, there is Kate, my daughter.
This book is for her, who opened my heart,
Creating a space for me to learn to Dwell.

I'm also grateful for Richard Dancy,
Our beloved priest,
Who helped me understand what is in the vision
That's calling me.
Richard died suddenly as I was in the middle of writing Dwelling;
He continued counseling me after he crossed over
And is still with me.

Dwelling is also for Henry, our grandson.
Dwelling burst into deeper realms while
Being with him (his parents live abroad).
He fills their home with Light and sweetness
Which flowed through my writing.
I pray his grandchildren will be able
 To read this book in good health.

To my parents, endless thanks
For giving me this life, and all of your love.
We came from different planets
Yet we are held by the same gravity.

Finally, all gratitude to my wife Beth
Who I explore Dwelling with daily.
My eternal partner is the other half
Of a splitting cell.
Our union is
The space lightning creates during a strike;
The edge of a wave flowing onto the beach, the moment
The ocean begins to draw back.
Our hope is the morning sun shining
Through a forest after a night of rain.

Writing Dwelling was a process
Of holding the door open,
Inviting friends to listen to The music
And sing with me.
Many voices filled the air, especially
Alice, Anne, Daniela, Emily, Lourdes
Sean, Bill, Dave and Keith.
I have all gratitude for you.

SOURCES

PHOTO CREDITS

Apropos of Dwelling being a community effort, my dear friend, Krista Schlyer, photographer and environmental/social activist, provided the core photos. Many of the images came from her book, *Continental Divide*, which she wrote to raise awareness of the environmental impact of the border wall.   kristaschlyer.com

Another friend, Angie Seckinger, provided the especially poetic "macro" images, which invite us deep within, to pay attention — to Dwell.   macrojourney.com

The portrait of me was taken by another dear friend, Tamzin Smith, a DC-area portrait photographer with a sensitive and insightful eye. tamzinsmithphoto.com

All other images came from Unsplash, a free photo website, where aspiring photographers post their work, to share with others — an extraordinary range of images. Thank you all.

BILL HUTCHINS is a poet and an architect, who tells stories through space and form. He founded Helicon Works Architects, a unique architectural collaborative community, in 1989, based in Takoma Park, MD, where he lived with his family until 2019.

Bill learned Dwelling during this time — his personal unfolding has informed his architectural work, as it gave him the eyes to see Dwelling. Bill has also developed Dwelling by working with clients in the making of their homes.

The creating and building of his family's home, completed in 2006, galvanized his understanding of Dwelling. This home is alive, playful, healing, with cozy spaces for intimate moments, and a luminous gathering room, where he and his wife shared their home for many events.

In 2019, Bill and Beth moved to her ancestral home — she's the fourth generation, in south-central Vermont, embedded in the Green Mountain National Forest — that they had previously renovated. Dwelling deepened as it mingled with two hundred years of posts and beams and stories. Now Bill also dwells through loving a forest, which he documented in the second Dwelling book, Learning to Love a Forest. You can peruse this second book on the Dwelling website.

Bill is also the Board President of a Nepalese foundation — www.KRMEF.org. In his role there he is helping to bring sustainable practices to the foundation's village just south of Kathmandu. This community is another family for Bill.

www.ingramcontent.com/pod-product-compliance
Lightning Source LLC
Chambersburg PA
CBHW080818120626
46556CB00010B/3323